Get Smarter!

GET SMARTER!

Mirjam Pol

Set Yourself Up for Study Success

VU University Press

VU University Press
De Boelelaan 1105
1081 HV Amsterdam
The Netherlands

www.vuuniversitypress.com
info@vuuniversitypress.nl

Cover and interior design:
Bas Smidt, 's-Gravenhage
Illustrations: Maaike Hartjes

ISBN 978 90 8659 847 2
NUR 143

© Mirjam Pol, 2021

All rights reserved.
No part of this book may be reproduced,
stored in a retrieval system, or transmitted,
in any form or by any means, electronic,
mechanical, photocopying, recording, or
otherwise, without the prior written
consent of the publisher.

TABLE OF CONTENTS

Did you know that...   6

1. Introduction   7
2. The Circle of Learning Success   11
3. Learning to study: try and see if it works   16
4. The working of the brain: connecting and adjusting   22
5. Mindset: what you think matters   30
6. Time management: why having a plan makes sense   39
7. Setting priorities   46
8. Concentrating   52
9. Overcoming procrastination   60
10. Motivation: how do you keep it up?   68
11. Mind maps   74
12. Mnemonics: tricks for training your memory   81
13. Exams: training for different types of exams   86
14. Taking exams: thriving on the right amount of stress   94
15. The pitfalls of a resit   102
16. Perseverance   108
17. Preconditions   117
18. A new action plan   122

Tips for books and videos   126

DID YOU KNOW THAT...

- Students who believe that talent and intelligence can be developed are best set up for study success.
- When you are motivated, your brain produces chemical substances that ensure that you retain the information better.
- Learning involves organising and reorganising the networks of nerve cells in your brain. You can guide this process through motivation, effort, repetition of the study material and pleasure.
- There are also ways in which you can positively influence your motivation.
- You remember more if you study in short blocks.
- The happier you are in your personal life, the better your study performance will be.
- If you are having personal problems, there are people at your university or faculty who can and want to help you.
- IQ is like the horsepower (HP) of a car. What good is it if you never take the car out of the garage? Success, whether in your studies or future career, depends to a great extent on how you use your HP.
- Understanding the form of an exam in advance allows you to get better grades without necessarily having to study more.
- Studying can be learned: it's all about skills and strategies.

1 INTRODUCTION

Hello student! This may sound strange, but did you know that you can learn how to study? That the way you think about yourself has a huge effect on your future performance? And that you can actively influence the creation of new brain networks, and thus improve your performance? These topics, and many more, are discussed in this book. It can help you to look at yourself in a new way and improve your study results. This book aims to maximise the potential that you have inside yourself. To do so, you need to learn to understand your typical responses, how you think (and how your thoughts are influenced by others), how your brain works, and what learning methods you can apply.

> **This may sound strange, but did you know that you can learn how to study?**

Who is this book intended for? It's for students who are interested in discovering effective and fast learning techniques. For students who spend a lot of time studying and would like to achieve the same results in less time. For students who got worse grades than they expected and would like to change that. And for students who have trouble getting started or have hit a brick wall in their studies.

1.1 Getting started

Most new students need time to get up to speed. You have to get used to your new environment, to writing papers, and to other ways of teaching and studying. You may have practical worries about how to survive on the money you have, where to live or how to find a new GP. It's only natural that you need time to adjust to your new situation. If you get stuck later on in your studies, it can be useful to do a quick scan to pinpoint the problem.

1.2 Quick scan: want-can-do

Do you feel stuck? Then start by asking yourself these questions. Don't I want to do it? Am I unable to do it? Or is it that I just won't do it? What exactly is the problem?

If you don't want to take this course, then it doesn't make sense to cram it all in. Sooner or later, you will have to face up to this fact. It makes more sense to properly explore your motivation. Did you have other expectations? Did your parents pressure you to choose this major? Deciding on what to study can be an exciting experience, but with so many choices, picking one course can be a difficult task. So, it's no wonder that so many students switch majors. What would you like to do most if you were to allow yourself to dream about it?

If you simply can't do something, then you need to add some skills to your toolkit. What exactly can't you do? Distinguish between main and side issues? Work according to a plan? Prioritise? Collaborate? Present your work? Make good summaries? All these skills can be learned! There is a good chance that your university offers training courses to develop these skills.

Do you want to do it and you are able to do it, but something is holding you back? Are you afraid to make mistakes? Do you find it difficult to get started? Or do you tend to put things off? You can work on these things, too. This book can show you how.

Looking at your situation from a want-can-do perspective can help you to determine what is going wrong for you. And from there, you can start looking for a suitable solution.

1.3 The behaviour of the driver is more important than the HP of the engine

Studying smarter is primarily a question of behaviour. Research shows that study success depends much more on behaviour than on intelligence. If you look at biographies of great inventors, musicians and athletes, you will see that most of them got to where they did by working with others, trying different things, learning from their mistakes, persevering when setbacks occurred, asking for help when they were unable to do something on their own, taking on challenges, and being open to suggestions from others.

It takes more than talent to be successful. Talent has to manifest itself, and this is where behaviour comes in. If you are aware of how your thoughts influence your behaviour, you can control your behaviour in an even smarter way. This will be discussed in more detail in this book. The trick is to use your intelligence properly. To use it smartly and, by doing so, to have more fun while studying.

2 THE CIRCLE OF LEARNING SUCCESS

Let's begin by looking at the learning process itself. It is a fairly logical process, with a fairly logical result: new brain networks. Learning involves establishing or extending the networks of nerve cells in your brain. If the networks are large and strong enough, you will pass your exam, give a good presentation or complete your internship successfully.

The good news is that establishing and strengthening these networks is a process that you can control. Repetition and application of the study material are key aspects in this respect. Motivation and pleasure also ensure that the organisation of these networks runs more smoothly and quickly.

2.1 The stages of the Circle of Learning Success

Establishing and strengthening brain networks is a step-by-step process. The Circle of Learning Success describes these stages clearly and logically.

1. Action plan
Create a clear plan before you begin studying. In this plan, you describe what your goals are, make an outline of the week or

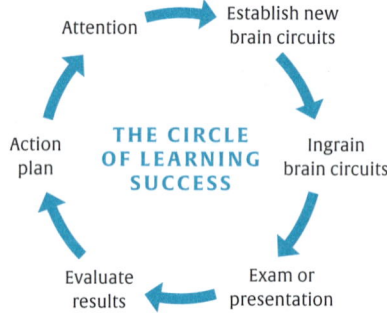

month and identify when you are going to do what, list which method you intend to use, and state what obstacles you expect to encounter and how you plan to resolve them. Useful chapters for this stage of the Circle of Learning Success are:
- Chapter 6, Time management: why having a plan makes sense
- Chapter 7, Setting priorities
- Chapter 17, Preconditions

2. Attention
Read the study material attentively. New brain circuits can only be established if you pay enough attention. If you can't pay attention, it is not worthwhile continuing to study. Concentration problems, test anxiety, procrastination and brooding are all problems that distract your attention and reduce your focus. It is also possible that are you are studying too much: when you pour over your books for hours, the parts of your brain that are important for learning switch to standby.
The following chapters provide more information on this stage of the Circle of Learning Success:

- Chapter 8, Concentrating
- Chapter 9, Overcoming procrastination
- Chapter 10, Motivation: how do you keep it up?
- Chapter 16, Perseverance

3. Establish new brain circuits

If you pay attention to something, brain circuits can be established. Existing networks can also be reorganised, for instance, because the new study material strengthens what you have already learned about a specific topic. As a result, pre-established circuits are expanded or slightly altered.

Establishing new networks requires effort. To do so successfully, it is especially important that you make an active and conscious effort to fully understand the new information. Otherwise, the new networks will be full of loose ends and will disappear easily or not function properly.

Certain study methods, such as mind maps and speed reading, can help to establish circuits, or make them faster or stronger. Mnemonics can also be useful in this respect. Useful chapters for this stage of the Circle of Learning Success are:
- Chapter 4, The working of the brain: connecting and adjusting
- Chapter 11, Mind maps
- Chapter 12, Mnemonics: tricks for training your memory

4. Ingrain brain circuits

Once a brain network has been established, it has to be strengthened. This can be done by reviewing the study material, applying it or explaining it out loud (or saying it to yourself in your head if you are in a library or other quiet space). A good night's sleep is also important during this stage. The networks

that you established during the day are reviewed many times as you sleep, which ensures the study material is even further ingrained. The following chapters provide useful information on this stage of the Circle of Learning Success:
- Chapter 4, The working of the brain: connecting and adjusting
- Chapter 17, Preconditions

5. Exam or presentation

It is possible that you paid enough attention, that the networks were well established and strengthened, but you still failed an exam or messed up your presentation. Ensuring that the stored information can be reproduced requires a special kind of skill. There are things you can do to increase the chance of successfully reproducing information. The following chapters tell you how:
- Chapter 13, Exams: training for different types of exams
- Chapter 14, Taking exams: thriving on the right amount of stress
- Chapter 15, The pitfalls of a resit

6. Evaluate results

If you have failed an exam or are disappointed with a result, it is worthwhile evaluating the exam or discussing the presentation with your tutor. This way, you can find out exactly what went wrong or why things did not go the way you hoped or expected. It is important to know what you don't understand. To do so, you need to turn frustration into positive energy. This stage is about perseverance, resilience, character and grit. Working on a growth mindset can help you with this. Useful chapters for this stage of the Circle of Learning Success are:

- Chapter 5, Mindset: what you think matters
- Chapter 16, Perseverance

7. New action plan

Once you find out in what areas your action plan could be improved, you can prepare a new plan. Keep the things that worked for you and change what did not. Chapter 18 can help you with this. You are now ready to take the first step.

2.2 Let's get started

How is this book structured? To get warmed up, read Chapter 3 to find out why it's important to try different methods of studying and to keep checking whether they are effective. In Chapter 4, we look at how the brain works. You will find out that everything in the brain revolves around making connections and adjustments.

After the basics have been covered, we move on to mindsets (Chapter 5). Mindsets are incredibly important for how you think about yourself and how you perform. After reviewing this chapter, you are ready to learn about the specific learning methods that are discussed in Chapter 6 to 14. By placing these methods and the topics of Chapters 15 to 17 in the Circle of Learning Success, they will be even more effective (Chapter 18). After you have finished reading this book, you will be equipped with strategies to study in a smarter way. This will not only empower you to get better results, but also make you feel better and allow you to build a solid foundation for a professional career. I hope you enjoy reading this book and draw inspiration from it!

3 LEARNING TO STUDY: TRY AND SEE IF IT WORKS

Before we begin, there is one thing I would like to point out. The way you learn at university differs from the way you learned in secondary school. There will be different subjects, fewer fixed hours and different teaching methods (e.g., study groups, tutorials, project-based teaching, lectures, internships, competency-oriented studying). You will have more freedom in many respects, but also more responsibility. The only person responsible for your success is you. This may take some getting used to, especially if you managed to get by with little effort until now.

3.1 What method works best for you?

Given all these changes, it is smart to discover what works for you. At the same time, it is equally important to find out what does not work. There is a simple rule that can help you with this:

> A person learns from trying and seeing if it works.

The American psychologist, professor and educational theorist Daniel Kolb has become famous by describing this process. Here's what it looks like:

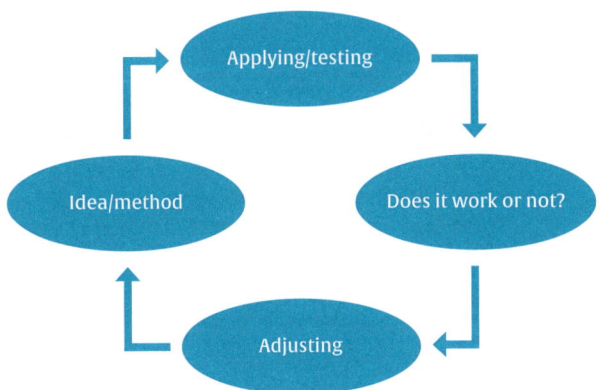

You probably have an idea what study method work best for you. Perhaps because it worked well for you before, like in secondary school. When you have to take a test now, it feels natural to use the same method again. If you pass your exam, you conclude that you are on the right track and don't have to change anything. But if you unexpectedly fail, then this is the moment to consider adjusting your study method.

By the way, the same applies if you passed but the grade was lower than expected. Or if you had to study for a long time in order to get a good grade or you did not enjoy the process leading up to the exam. In all of these cases, adjusting your strategy is the smarter option. This means you think of a new way of approach, try it out and evaluate it. Success and failure are both learning experiences. It's what you do afterwards with what you have learned that counts.

3.2 Stop muddling on

The first step in a new direction can be quite difficult. We tend to prefer to leave things as they are and muddle on. Do the statements below sound like you?
- 'How can I be sure that a different method will work?'
- 'If it doesn't work, I will have wasted all that time I invested.'
- 'A new method takes too much time to get used to, and I can't afford to lose time.'

These types of reactions are the result of insecurity, possibly caused by unpleasant experiences with change you have had in the past. This may have caused you to draw conclusions which confirm your fears ('See, it's pointless to...'). It is also possible to feel uncertain or scared even if you did not have any unpleasant experiences with change in the past.

Another common reason for muddling along is, 'I need to be able to do it myself'. This can be viewed in two ways. On a positive note, you don't give up easily and are willing to get help. Good for you! However, if this way of thinking is stopping you from making changes that benefit you, this behaviour is not doing you any good. It is causing you to go round in circles and keeping you from progressing. If this is the case, you should ask for help. It may be reassuring to know that being flexible and arranging the right help in time is a professional skill.

3.3 Do you dare to invest in a new method?

Finding a new method of studying can be a struggle and may feel like you are muddling along. Don't be too hard on yourself. Investing in a new method takes time in the beginning. It's OK if you have to get used to it. It's different from muddling along because you are reflecting on your own behaviour. You have thought about what was missing or didn't work. You have chosen a new method of studying and decided to try it out. And you are going to evaluate whether the new method is effective, both in terms of time and result. If it isn't, you go around the circle again: adjust, think of a new method, try it out, check whether it works, etc. This is called perseverance, not muddling along. When you are muddling along, you are not reflecting on what you do or checking what works and what doesn't.

Academic studying can be compared to learning a new sport. Take, for instance, judo. Judo involves technique, creativity, lots of practice and perseverance. The final goal is to get the study material 'on the mat'. In other words, to assimilate and apply what you have learned.

To conclude this chapter, here are five myths that you need to stop believing.

Myth 1: 'Everyone gets it except me, so I better keep quiet'
Are you comparing yourself to others and feeling like you are not measuring up? Remember that if you are struggling with a problem, chances are others are too. However stupid you feel or afraid you are of something, rest assured you are not the only one feeling this way! Your study adviser can confirm this. Trying to pretend that nothing is wrong will not solve the problem. Take action.

Myth 2: 'I can do it all by myself'
Some students wait too long before they ask for help. They want to or feel that they should be able to solve the problem on their own. There is nothing wrong with being self-sufficient, as long as you can manage and are making progress. But it is equally important to ask for help when you can't manage on your own. Getting the right help promptly is an important professional skill.

Myth 3: 'There's nothing wrong with being cocky in a good way'
That's true, as long as it works. But if being cocky means getting poor grades, you would be wise to take a different approach.

Myth 4: 'I have to get in the flow first'
Being in a state of flow means that you are able to focus on your studies for a long period, perhaps even for hours, with interest and pleasure. Who wouldn't want that? But you should not become fixated on flow. Professionals can't afford to have their performance depend on something so elusive. If you want to excel in the career you are studying for, you don't need flow, but rather time, effort, commitment and perseverance.

Myth 5: 'That's just the way I am'

Change is part of our existence on this planet. Nothing in the universe remains the same. This applies to you, too. However, although change is inevitable, this does not mean it is effortless. Changing your thoughts, feelings or behaviour takes time and hard work. This is because you need to establish new networks or reorganise existing networks in your brain. This can take weeks or even months. Creating a path across a field is easy, but building a new motorway takes much longer. The good news is that you can change by taking one step at a time, with help from others and many rewards along the way. With self-awareness, willpower and creative imagination, you can be certain that your motorway will be built.

4 THE WORKING OF THE BRAIN: CONNECTING AND ADJUSTING

One thing is clear: you will be using your brain differently from what you've been used to in secondary school. Did you ever think about the three pounds of brain inside your skull and what exactly is happening up there? It's busy networking. The brain is all about networks.

When you learn something, you can see that reflected physically in your brain: nerve cells establish new networks, or they reorganise existing networks. This is what we call learning. Learning is nothing more or less than the organisation and reorganisation of networks of cooperating nerve cells.

> **The brain consists of a hundred billion nerve cells (neurons)**

The brain consists of a hundred billion nerve cells (neurons). They can form trillions of connections. That offers quite a perspective! And the best part is that you can guide the formation of these networks through practice, repetition, motivation and pleasure.

But before we get to that, let's take a look at the basics.

4.1 Every time we learn something new our brain forms new connections

The nerve cells form the most essential components of the brain. Nerve cells come in different shapes and sizes, but their basic design is the same. Each nerve cell has a so-called cell body. At the bottom there is the axon, which is long and thick. Extending from the cell body are the dendrites, the receivers, which are thin and highly branched. They receive electrochemical signals from other nerve cells and pass them along.

When you learn something new, the number of dendrites increases, and so does the number of receivers. The more receivers there are, the bigger or faster the network will be, which comes in handy when you are taking an exam or giving a presentation.

4.2 You can influence the organisation and reorganisation of networks in your brain

The structure of your brain literally changes through studying. New connections are made. New networks are created, and existing networks are strengthened, expanded or made faster. Now that you know this, you can use this to your advantage.

First of all, make sure that you understand what you are learning. If you do not understand the study material, you will end up with a muddled and weak network or no network at all. How do you make sure that you get it? And how can you check yourself? Leaf through the previous pages. Find a You-

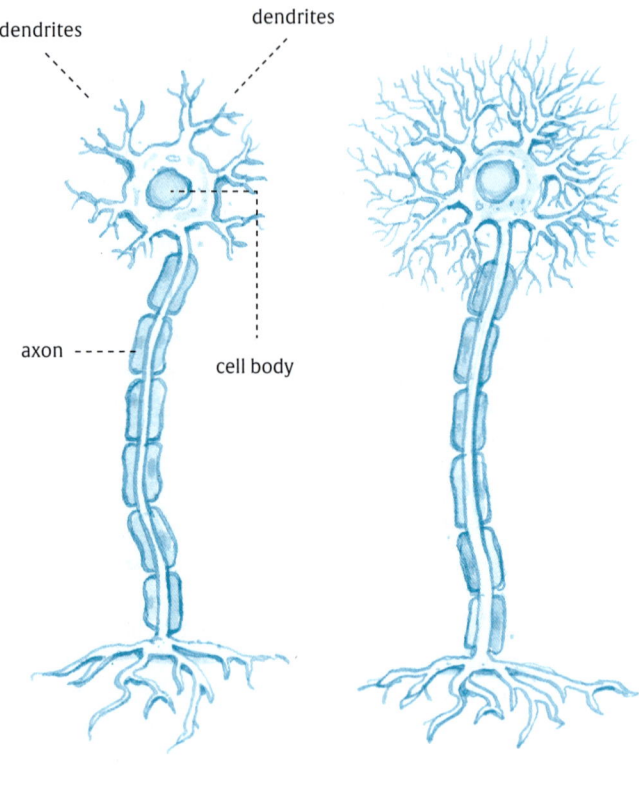

BEFORE LEARNING   AFTER LEARNING

Tube video that explains it. Talk to fellow students. Create a mind map (see Chapter 11). The most important tip: ask questions! Good ways to start a question are:
- How can that… / How is it possible that… / How does it work if… / How should…?
- Why is it that… / Why is that it isn't…?
- When…?
- What are the most important things that you should do?

Search actively for answers in the study material. This will allow you to understand and remember the information better.

Don't study too long or not enough: between 20 and 45 minutes at a stretch is a good guideline. The brain needs time to process all the information it receives. It checks whether it recognises the information, decides where it belongs, in what order it should be stored, etc. If you don't study long enough, you don't generate enough momentum to understand complicated matters. On the other hand, if you study too long your brain becomes overloaded and can no longer process new information.

> **Don't study too long or not enough**

Therefore, it is important to incorporate short breaks. This will allow the brain to process the incoming information better and faster. Let your brain catch its breath! Sometimes a four-minute break will do the trick, sometimes you may need an hour. Eventually, you will get a feel for it and know exactly when to stop because new information is no longer being processed.

How long should you study before taking a break? This varies from one situation to the next. If you don't find the study material very interesting and you're hungry, then your brain will stop organising or reorganising networks sooner. If you are engaged, enjoying yourself and your stomach is full, then you will be able to study longer. If you notice that you are distracted – and you may not be aware of this so be sure to check yourself every so often – look at the study material and decide what you want to accomplish or how long you want to keep going. This way, you can train yourself to be focused and you can continue to control your concentration.

So, the two important preconditions for studying effectively are to really understand the study material and to make sure you don't study too long or for too short a time. Here are three more tips to positively influence your brain and achieve the results you want.

1. Focus

You can only build or expand networks if you focus your full attention on the study material. How do you do that?
- Mute smartphones and tablets and keep them out of sight. Close the door.
- Work in a tidy environment. A cluttered, messy room will affect your ability to focus and concentrate, even if you are not aware of it, because your eyes register all this information. Seeing other things, however briefly or unconsciously, costs working memory capacity. What a waste!

In Chapter 8 and 9, concentration and procrastination are discussed in more detail.

2. Use your brain chemistry	When you are motivated, your brain produces dopamine. Dopamine is a chemical substance, a neurotransmitter, that helps us retain new information. It is literally used to build better networks. So, it makes sense to work on your motivation! However, if you are stressed – mind you, boredom is also a form of stress – then the electricity in your brain networks generates neurotransmitters that cause an unpleasant feeling and affect your ability to study. Chapter 12 discusses motivation and how to stay motivated in more detail.
3. Make it fun	'NEW!' and 'FUN!' are like sweets for the brain. And the brain certainly loves sweet treats. But what if the study material is boring or sleep inducing? In that case, it is up to you to spice things up. Look for new information that says the same thing but in a new and engaging way. This can be books, videos or MOOCs, or conversations with interesting people from the field – anything to get your mind to spark.

4.3 Repetition and application are important

There are different ways of guiding the organisation and reorganisation of networks in your brain. Here's a final tip to really strengthen your network: repeat, repeat, repeat and repeat! The following three moments in the learning process are especially suited for repetition.

1. When you start studying	Make use of what you already know and incorporate recaps. This 'wakes up' existing networks that are linked to the new study material, while the older networks offer a basis for the new information. This makes sense because it takes less effort to expand existing networks than to create entirely new ones. What's more, the older networks also help you to understand and retain the new information faster and better. So when you start a particular topic or a new assignment be sure to actively recall what you already know about it. Leaf back through the pages and go through your notes, even it was just a short while ago.
2. When you finish studying	Routinely reserve two to three minutes at the end of each study period to review the information. Make a habit of repeating the material out loud or saying it to yourself in your mind. This will allow you to further ingrain the information. There is also another, equally important, benefit. If you can explain the study material out loud, this means there is a good foundation for the network. So, repeating out loud allows you to see how well you have retained the information.
3. At the end of the week	Schedule 90 minutes of review time at the end of each week. Use this time to summarise all the material and to make connections. This will improve your insight. You can also do some additional exercises to see if you still understand the material. The more you use your nerve network, the stronger it becomes. Use it or lose it! By reviewing and applying the material, you optimally prepare your network for an exam or a presentation.

If you don't have time to review or apply the study material, then take a close look at your schedule (see Chapter 6, Time management). It would be a pity if the networks you created are not strong enough for you to pass the exam. Repetition is an essential part of this. If you plan smartly and perhaps set new priorities, you will have time for reviewing. It is also possible that you spend too much time cramming or reading. In that case, a course in speed reading, mind mapping or memory techniques can be useful. Most universities offer these courses.

5 MINDSET: WHAT YOU THINK MATTERS

It all boils down to making connections and adjusting them. This is how you create networks in your brain and retain information. But does this require self-confidence?

Self-confidence is not the obvious key to success. Not every extremely self-confident person gets good grades. And sometimes you get good grades without feeling overly confident. What is important is that you can re-examine your thoughts when you are confronted with obstacles, such as disappointing results. What do we mean by thoughts? Ideas about what kind of student you are. Do you think, 'This is the way I am and that's it'?, or do you see yourself as someone who is open to change? These questions have to do with your mindset. There are roughly to types of mindsets: a fixed mindset and a growth mindset.

> Do you think, 'This is the way I am and that's it'?

5.1 Two types of mindsets

Do you think you can change your intelligence or talent? This question lies at the heart of the distinction between a fixed and a growth mindset. The conviction that intelligence or talent can't change is called a fixed mindset, whereas the conviction that you can develop intelligence and talent is called a growth mindset. Below are some typical statements that clarify both mindsets.

Fixed mindset	• You're either smart or you're not, people are just the way they are. • If you don't have any talent, it is better not to do certain things.
Growth mindset	• Practice and effort will get you far. • Everybody can always have new experiences. • A person keeps changing their whole life long.

Students with a fixed mindset are more strongly influenced by what others think of them than students with a growth mindset. Students with a growth mindset are more focused on how they can improve themselves.

5.2 The effect of a mindset

A mindset influences your feelings and your behaviour. Some of the known effects are presented in the table below.

	Students with a fixed mindset...	**Students with a growth mindset...**
Feelings	... often feel less relaxed. They are always asking themselves, Am I doing it right? Am I smart enough?	... feel happier and more relaxed. They are curious.
Motivation	... who feel that they do not have enough talent are not motivated to work hard. After all, what's the point? Students who believe they are talented are extremely motivated to work hard. They want to show how good or smart they are.	... are highly motivated, whether the task is difficult or simple.
Dealing with obstacles	... quickly give up when confronted with obstacles. They avoid confrontation out of fear of disapproval or rejection.	... persevere when confronted with obstacles.
Dealing with challenges	... avoid challenges. Either you are good at something or you are not. Challenges are threatening. What if you fail? People will think you are stupid. It's best not to go there.	... relish challenges. More than anything, they want to discover and learn.

	Students with a fixed mindset...	**Students with a growth mindset...**
Dealing with feedback	... prefer not to get feedback.	... may be startled at first, but then say, 'Bring it on'. Sometimes even, 'Great! Yes, please!'
Dealing with success of others	... prefer to compare themselves with students or people who are doing worse than they are. This makes them look smarter.	... prefer to compare themselves with students or people who have progressed further than they have. They can learn from them.
Making an effort	... think that making an effort is virtually pointless. Either you are smart, or you are stupid, the amount of effort you put in is not going to change that.	... think that making an effort always pays off. You can always get better or learn something new. Of course, not everyone can become a genius, but you can improve and grow.

5.3 Where do mindsets come from?

Mindsets originate from two major sources: the messages we get from our parents and our teachers. A fixed mindset can have a positive or a negative variant. In the latter case, parents or teachers literally tell you that you are stupid or not smart enough. Or they predict that you will never succeed at anything. It is possible that they say these things to protect you. These messages don't have to be explicit. Most often, you can guess what people are thinking from their attitude or body language.

In the positive variant, teachers or parents compliment you on how clever you are, how smart and quick, and how much you can achieve even with little effort. While their intentions are good, the effect is detrimental. The message you are getting is that you are smart, instead of learning that hard work and *the right skills and strategies* will get you far. After all, that is the intention of parents and teachers who think in terms of growth and change. They want to stimulate you to think of every situation as an opportunity. A chance to discover how you can develop yourself even further, keep growing and learn something new.

5.4 Think helpful thoughts

Your thoughts are your thoughts, and there's nothing wrong with that. But you also need to be aware of the effects of your thoughts on your attitude and your behaviour. It is extremely important to use your brain not only to study, but also to reflect on yourself, on what you are doing, and on what you are not doing or perhaps should be doing. How are you going about your studies? If you notice for the first time that you really need to put in an effort in order to achieve something, do you dare to do that? If you are used to succeeding without much effort and now you're getting bad grades, do you have the courage to try a new method? If you fall flat on your face, do you focus on self-pity, shame, and a feeling of having failed? Or do you get up and think, 'What can I learn from this?', even if it hurts?

Your thoughts can help you to get up and keep at it. To persevere. To become resilient. But they can also get in your way. Ask yourself these questions to find out for yourself whether your thoughts help you when your study results are disappointing, or cause you to quit rather than persevere? To copy answers rather than study the material in depth? To slam your book shut rather than ask a teacher for help?

> **Your thoughts can help you to get up and keep at it**

If you find out that your thoughts are actually hindering you, then do something about it. After all, you are more than your thoughts. It won't be easy, but it can be done. You can learn to think differently.

5.5 Six tips to think positive thoughts

You can change a mindset. By thinking different thoughts, you build other networks. These new networks will make you feel different, because new networks form a new pattern of chemical substances. And when you feel different, you will start to behave differently. Mind you, it takes time to change networks, to create new neural pathways. You can't build a new motorway in a few days either.

If your convictions are not serving you and you want to change them, the following tips can help you. They all have one thing in common: think positively!

Think positively 1	If something doesn't work out, analyse which skill or strategy can help you to succeed next time.
Think positively 2	If something doesn't work out, think about things that you have done well. You put in a lot of effort, chose an effective partial strategy, showed initiative, put yourself out there, etc. Compliment yourself for that.
Think positively 3	Pay yourself a compliment when something does work out. Focus on the effort you made or your strategy: 'You worked hard!' or 'Good choice!'.
Think positively 4	If other people fail to achieve something, make a conscious effort to find something that they did do well (e.g., effort, initiative, daring). Compliment them for that and support them in analysing their skills or strategies.

Think positively 5	If something works out for other people, congratulate them and ask them how they did it.
Think positively 6	Ask people you trust to provide feedback. What did you do well? Is there anything you could have done differently?

5.6 Special tip: think about one of your heroes

Something that always does the trick is to think about someone you admire. Who is your role model when it comes to a growth mindset? This could be someone you know personally, or a celebrity, a top athlete, a DJ, an artist or an inventor. Let this person inspire you. How did they deal with setbacks or challenges? How did they handle the mistakes they made? Whenever you are having a hard time, think about what they would do or think. What challenges did they take on without knowing whether they would succeed? And what did they do when things didn't work out or they made a mistake? Can't think of a role model? Then make someone up. It is just as effective.

5.7 To conclude: mindset and (intellectual) giftedness

In elementary and secondary school, gifted children are often praised for being smart. The result is that 'being smart' becomes part of their identities. Students who were labelled as smart in elementary or secondary school are more vulnerable later on when dealing with setbacks. If you think in terms of clever or stupid (fixed mindset), you tend to interpret setbacks as failures. As 'being stupid'. It may cause you to cut corners or stop preparing for tests. This has two benefits. If you pass the exam anyway, this confirms how smart you are, which is nice. And if you fail, you can always say, 'That was to be expected because I didn't prepare'.

These students aren't dozy or lazy. They are showing avoidance behaviour because their identity is under threat. They are afraid they will no longer be appreciated. They are not, or not yet, accustomed to challenges, hard work, actively searching for patterns or feedback from others. The relevant networks to deal with all this still have to be formed or are not yet fully developed in their brain. In addition, most bright students tend to make obvious study choices. If you are good at mathematics, then studying mathematics is a logical choice. But the fact that you found a particular subject easy in secondary school does not necessarily mean that you like it. Or that studying it at a higher or different level automatically ensures success. Does this sound like you? Then first find out what motivates you. After that you can focus on developing a growth mindset.

> **The result is that 'being smart' becomes part of their identities**

6 TIME MANAGEMENT: WHY HAVING A PLAN MAKES SENSE

There are various techniques for retaining information, such as setting priorities, mind mapping, memory techniques, and learning how to deal with procrastination, or loss of concentration or motivation. All these topics will be covered in the following chapters. But let's start with something most students enjoy: making a plan. Yes!

Don't worry, you don't have to make a plan. Just as with all the other topics in this book, the adage 'if it works, it works' applies. And if it doesn't, that's perfectly fine. But you can only find this out by experimenting.

Personally, I'm a huge fan of making a plan. This is because I have seen time and again that it works. Having a well-defined study plan gives you peace of mind. It can also be a wonderful instrument to make clever use of your time, to get better results, or to boost your happiness while studying. So, I encourage everyone to at least try it.

There are several planning methods. Below we will elaborate on one method. Your study adviser will be able to show your other methods that could be right for you.

6.1 Goals and benefits of a plan

One of the most important goals of a plan is to gain an overview. Once you have an overview, you will feel calmer and more self-confident. This alone is a benefit for most students. Other goals could be reducing procrastination or problems with concentration and self-discipline.

The four benefits of a plan are:

Benefit 1	You learn to estimate what has to be done in the near future (getting a clear idea of expectations).
Benefit 2	You learn what will be covered in the module or term (distinguishing between main and secondary issues).
Benefit 3	You learn what you need to do each day (estimating the difficulty of the material and your own efforts).
Benefit 4	You get to know yourself well. Are you overestimating your abilities or underestimating the difficulty of the material? Or vice versa? Are you studying too hard or too little? What events or thoughts are keeping you from your plan? What priorities do you set when you get stuck?

All these skills will be very useful to you later, no matter what field you end up in. One essential condition is that the plan must be right for you, otherwise you won't be able to carry it out. Below I will talk about how you can make a plan that suits your needs.

6.2 Time management in five steps

Step 1. Schedule fun things
- Establish how many weeks you will need to prepare for the exam.
- Use a single landscape page for each week. Divide it into seven days, with three sections per day. Preferably on the computer, so you don't have to erase entries when your plan falls apart or you have to revise it.
- Decide which weekends, evenings, days or hours you will spend on personal matters (e.g., sports, jobs, parties, friends, relationship, outings, hobbies). Schedule time for these matters first.
- Make sure you have a least one study-free day a week, so you have time to relax.

Step 2. Schedule obligatory or essential course components
- Fill in your study groups or work groups, project meetings, lectures, labs, internship or other course components.

Step 3. Make an estimate of the material and divide it up
- Your brain can only concentrate well for an average of 20 to 45 minutes at a time. After that, it needs to process all the input it has received before it can attend to processing new information. Determine how long you can effectively study without stopping. This will be the length of one study block.
- Put all books, syllabi and other study material on a table. For each part, determine how many pages you think you

can study in one study block. If you have no idea, try studying for 30 minutes.
- On the basis of this estimate, calculate how many study blocks you will need in total. If you have to learn 100 pages of book A and it takes you 30 minutes to do 10 pages, then you will need 10 study blocks for that book. Do this for all your books and study materials. Let's assume you need a total of 46 study blocks of 30 minutes. Then number each block from 1 to 46.
- Schedule these study blocks. Think logically: if blocks 4 to 10 are a preparation for the Tuesday lecture, then schedule them for Monday or earlier.
- Alternate study activities such as learning, reading, making notes, preparing for a work group, working out sums, doing labs and creating a mind map. It is easier to spend more hours studying if you mix different types of activities.
- Tip: plan the right activity at the right time. For example, don't go shopping when your brain is at its best or don't plan to study a difficult text immediately after lunch.

Step 4. Incorporate reviews, spare time and practice exams

- Reserve 60 to 90 minutes a week for reviewing. If you don't review, you won't build strong brain circuits! If you 'don't have time' to review, you need to take a hard look at your priorities and rearrange your study schedule (see Chapter 7).
- Reserve two hours of spare time per week. This gives you enough flexibility to adjust your schedule partway through a week. If your plan is on the mark, you will have this time

to do a leisure activity. Saturday is generally a good day for that.
- Plan to do a practice exam halfway through your study block. Evaluate the result to make sure you are on the right path.
- Plan a second practice exam a few days before the actual exam. This way, you can check if you have also mastered the material that needed extra attention.
- If your schedule allows, incorporate some time for relaxation or revising the day before the exam. Do not learn new material during this time!

Step 5. Take a critical look
Go over your plan critically and ask yourself the following questions.
- Is my plan realistic? For example, did you include travel time?
- Is my plan feasible? If you know that you can't concentrate after 8.00 p.m., then don't plan any study activities in the evening.
- Is my plan balanced? Are the days equally intensive in terms of study load? Are they varied enough? If you are dreading certain days in your schedule, this will limit your chances of success. This doesn't mean that your days can't be completely filled or tough and you will probably enjoy some days more than others. But spreading the difficult bits evenly over the weeks will make your plan more manageable. Whatever you do, don't put them off!

If necessary, adjust your plan to make it feasible and doable. This could mean postponing personal matters so that you can study.

6.3 Know yourself

A plan is an intention committed to paper. Creating a plan and sticking to it requires self-knowledge and self-discipline. And the conviction that it will give you insight, peace of mind, and support the process of studying.

Self-knowledge means that you are able to determine when you need help. It does not mean that you can do everything yourself. If self-discipline is an issue for you, arranging study dates with someone who is very disciplined might be a good idea. Or prepare a plan with your study adviser and evaluate regularly how it is going. Do whatever is needed to be able to follow your plan.

6.4 Keep track of whether the plan works

Make a quick note on your plan when you are having trouble with a specific part of the material. Look at your notes at the end of the week. Is there a pattern that you can identify? Perhaps you can see a pattern in terms of time, study activity or reason. Here are a few examples to help you along.

- Time: Do problems occur primarily on Fridays? Or on days that you've had a lecture? Or in the evening?
- Study activity: What activity is affected first? For example, can you manage the reading but find it difficult to continue with the assignments?
- Reason: Do you tend to get stuck when your friends come around? Or because you are tired or don't feel like studying? Or are you too nonchalant about it?

You notes may reveal other reasons, such as:
- You plan too optimistically. You think you can do more things in a week than there are hours.
- You keep delaying or postponing your plan (procrastination).
- You feel resistance to obligations.

This kind of evaluation is important. The better you understand what is going on, the better equipped you will be to do something about it. Adjusting your plan based on self-knowledge and experience will only make your study plans better, which in turn will lead to many other benefits. For example, a balanced plan will allow you to combine studying with sports activities, activities with family and friends, or other exciting study projects.

7 SETTING PRIORITIES

What is important is seldom urgent, and what is urgent is seldom important.
– DWIGHT EISENHOWER

You may notice that you can't fit everything into your plan. Your plan may be packed with too many activities, such as study dates, a second major, activities with friends, committees, voluntary work, caring for a close relative, sports activities or clubbing. Balancing all these things at once can be exhilarating. Being busy, busy, busy gives you energy and makes you feel important. But there is a downside to filling your schedule to the brim. You will inevitably get very tired and stressed.

Imagine having your weekly schedule in front of you. You have indicated what activity you will be doing every 30 minutes. Your schedule is completely filled. Now do this: take an orange marker and highlight activities that are important as well as urgent.

The result? Most likely the page will be covered in orange. Because most students believe that most activities are both important and urgent. But that's not possible. You will go mad!

So, how is it possible that your entire plan is orange? Perhaps you have not yet learned the difference between important and urgent. Or stress could be temporarily clouding your ability to prioritise. Stress does this to us. It makes us lose sight of our goals and makes us less flexible and creative. Stress reduces the neural activity in areas of the brain that are responsible for this, while this neural activity is precisely what you need right now.

7.1 The Eisenhower Matrix

What should you do? You can follow Eisenhower's example. Eisenhower was the 34th president of the United States, served as Supreme Commander of the Allied forces during World War II, and was an avid golfer and accomplished amateur artist. He was known for being incredibly productive and extremely effective in terms of getting things done. His trick? His ability to distinguish. Eisenhower was the Priority King. He knew the difference between what was important and what wasn't, and what was urgent and what wasn't. This formed the basis for his actions. The model that he designed and therefore bears the name 'The Eisenhower Matrix' consists of four quadrants:

	Urgent	Not urgent
Important	1	2
Not important	3	4

Quadrant 1. Important and urgent
You need to get someone out of a burning building, your landlord calls you in a rage because you haven't paid the rent for months, or there's a mouse plague in your home, a huge family fight or a really important deadline. How do you handle it? There's no question about it, you simply do it! Determine what you need to deal with the situation. For example, help from others, a plan or drastic measures.

Quadrant 2. Important but not urgent
Friends, relationships, education, preparing for presentations or exams. But also, relaxation, commitment, contributing to your environment, your health. These things are all very important but not urgent. This quadrant is where you will spend the most time. Learn to focus on these goals and tasks.

Quadrant 3. Not important but urgent
This is everything you believe to be 'important'. In other words, most telephone calls, interruptions and distractions. This quadrant is also called 'the deception area'. We pretend these tasks have urgency, but they aren't truly important to the outcomes you are working toward. They are deceptive in that we like the excitement, the sense of urgency and the feeling of mattering. But if you look more closely, these tasks are not that important at all. What you should do is avoid them as much as possible. Challenge yourself to do so.

Quadrant 4. Not important and not urgent
This quadrant of the matrix is home to superfluous tasks. Activities that are nonsensical or a waste. It's also called the escape quadrant. We get caught up in these escapist activities

because we think they are relaxing. This is an illusion. They are a waste of time and will suck the productivity out of you. You need to stop going them! This will give you more air. If you minimise the amount of time you spend on tasks in this quadrant, you will have more time to relax. And more energy to focus on tasks in the second quadrant.

To summarise:

	Urgent	Not urgent
Important	Manage	Focus
Not important	Avoid	Limit

Keep track of how much time you spend in each quadrant. How is your weekly plan coming along? Can you afford to keep it as it is, or do you need take action to make your plan more realistic?

Is your schedule filled to the brim and threatening to overwhelm you because new, unexpected tasks are presenting themselves? Then follow Eisenhower's example.
1. Choose: to which quadrant can you assign the task?
2. Act: manage, focus, avoid or limit.

Is your schedule still too full or your life too busy? Then reach out to a counsellor or study adviser for help with organising and making decisions. You don't have to get it right the first time. This takes time to learn, so it is OK to practise.

7.2 What if quadrant 2 is overloaded?

What happens if avoiding quadrant 3 tasks and limiting quadrant 4 tasks does not free up enough of your time? What do you do when you have too many important activities? Then perhaps one of these situations applies to you:

- You have become trapped in success formulas. You believe that these thoughts are true and 100% accurate:
  - *I will never get a good job if I'm not on a committee.*
  - *I will never get a good job if I don't do a second major.*
  - *I will never be hired by that company if I don't pursue a PhD first.*
  - *She is my ticket to the future. If I don't do this for her, then ...'*

  Wake-up call: there are no success formulas! In fact, these types of thoughts are mostly false. If everyone were to follow the 'success formula', it wouldn't be a success formula, would it? After all, there are students who go on to big things without falling into this trap. There are also students who do everything by the book and fail to be successful. And there are students who discover that so-called success formulas don't make them happy at all. Life is not predictable, nor makeable. Tip: stop doing it. Create your life from a place of pleasure, knowing that step by step you will get to where you want to be.

> There are also students who do everything by the book and fail to be successful

- You are a perfectionist. You spend too much time on everything, because you want everything to be perfect, down to the smallest detail. Tip: read my book *From Stress*

to Success to turn perfectionism into healthy striving and to set attainable goals for yourself.
- You don't take enough breaks or are not fully present in the moment when you do something. You feel restless and agitated all the time. It is not so much the number of activities that causes you to feel overloaded, but rather the way you carry out these activities. When you learn to ride the waves that come into your life, you will gain more head space and heart space. You can't stop the waves, but you can learn to surf. Want to learn how? Read *Time Surfing* by Paul Loomans.
- You are taking care of a family member who is ill, which costs great deal of time and energy. Or you have taken on a job alongside your studies, because your parents expect you to or can't afford to put you through college. Tip: talk to your student counsellor. You could be eligible for financial support if you take longer to complete your studies than originally planned. Your counsellor can also help you find a study method or a plan that works better for your situation.
- You have a disability or chronic disease. Educational institutions have a duty of care to do everything they can, so far as is reasonably practicable, to provide for the well-being of students. This means you may qualify for financial support. Your student counsellor will be able to advise you on this and provide practical support.

The ability to distinguish between what is important and what isn't important or urgent is a skill. You can train this skill and learn to act accordingly. This will make you feel more relaxed and allow you to get more work done.

8 CONCENTRATING

We've covered the basics. The plan is in place. Perhaps you've even limited your plan to what is practical considering your schedule. It's time to get started! You get out your books, syllabus and laptop. You feel ready. But then you're distracted. The material may be less interesting than you expected. Or your mind keeps drifting off, no matter how hard you try. In other words, you are having trouble concentrating.

If you can't pay attention, you can't establish, expand or strengthen networks in your brain. So, continuing to study is not worthwhile. Try to figure out what the problem is and solve it. Then you can go back to studying.

8.1 Reasons for loss of concentration and possible solutions

There are many causes of loss of concentration. If there is a problem at this stage of the Circle of Learning Success, it is not possible to go on to the next step. Therefore, you should find out what the problem is and what you can do to solve it.

Reasons for loss of concentration	Possible solutions
You let yourself get distracted too much by fun things or friends.	Make clear agreements with yourself and your friends. Learn to say 'no'. Make a timetable to see if you can permit yourself time off for distractions with friends. Look for another place to study. Make sure you are not online.
You are a chronic multitasker.	Biologically, our brain is incapable of doing two things at the same time which both require serious attention. Multitasking is possible for simple things, such as walking and thinking or drinking and scrolling, but this doesn't apply to complex tasks. It is not a good idea, for instance, to study while checking your social media. Research shows this will result in poorer and slower performance in both areas. This is because, without you being aware of it, the brain switches between tasks extremely quickly and you're not aware of the amount of energy this requires. Nevertheless, the act of multitasking gives us a sense of satisfaction and achievement. We are therefore not suggesting that you get rid of it entirely, but rather that you turn off all your social media notifications and keep devices out of sight. Make an agreement with yourself which study tasks require your full attention and which ones can be multitasked.
You do not like a particular part of your course.	Make it fun! Find a way to jazz up the material. Because when you enjoy what you are doing, you will understand the material faster, studying will take less time, and you will build stronger networks! See Chapter 12 for more tips.

There are actually many parts of your course that you don't like.	Go see a career counsellor. Perhaps this is not the right course for you.
You regularly zone out without noticing it.	Shorten your study periods if you notice that you can't hold your attention. Start training yourself to improve your concentration span slowly by adding a few minutes every day to your study routine.
You feel the study material is too difficult.	Talk to a teacher, mentor or course coordinator, or look for materials such as books, websites, texts or videos that explain the subject in a different way.
You have personal problems.	If you have personal problems, it can be more difficult to concentrate on study assignments because you are carrying so much in your head and your heart. In that case, try a delaying tactic. Reserve time to deal with personal issues every day, say between 7.00 and 8.00 p.m. If any thoughts creep up at other times during the day, address them by saying, 'I hear you and I see you, and I'll pay attention to you at 7.00 p.m.' If these thoughts are very persistent, write them down as literally as possible and then address them again in the same way. Or move the time to deal with personal matters to an earlier time slot. During that time, which can range from 15 minutes to an hour, you can take action to resolve your personal problems. For example, by writing something down, organising your thoughts or discussing your situation with someone you trust.

8.2 Energy management

Many students want to banish the thoughts in their mind that are causing them to lose focus. But it doesn't work like that. Why? Because these thoughts are part of you. It is pointless to think, 'Leave me alone', 'Let me study' or 'I hate when I...'. If you are fighting against yourself, you are fighting a losing battle. What you can do, though, is manage your thoughts. This is called energy management, which is a nice term for self-control.

The starting point in energy management is that you accept that every part of you is OK. Even the parts that don't want to study all the time, want to put things off or want to have fun. However, there is only one person in charge who determines which part gets to say what and when – and that is you. It's about managing, not repressing.

The following absurd, yet very effective, exercise gives you an idea of how this can be accomplished. It will help you take charge of your own mind. The first step is to get to know the main players. After all, if you don't know who you are dealing with, you won't have anything to manage.

Exercise – The Round Table: who is doing the talking?

Sit in a quiet place where you will not be disturbed for the next 20 minutes. Imagine that you are sitting at the head of a large wooden table in a beautiful castle hall.

Make a list of what you want to do or achieve. For example, I want to play sports, keep my parents happy, pass my exam, see my friends on a regular basis, visit Barcelona, show people how good I am, etc. Number your wishes randomly.

Imagine wish number 1 is a man, woman or child and invite them to come in and sit at the table. (Don't overthink it, just do the first thing that comes to mind!) Take a good look at this person. What does he or she look like? What impression do you get from him or her?

Ask the person three questions:
1. How long have you been with me?
2. What is your intention? What do you ultimately want to achieve?
3. What is your approach?

Write down the answers. Invite wish number 2 and do the same. What is your first impression: a man, a woman or a child? Take a

---

good look at this person. Ask the same questions and write down the answers. Continue until there are no more wishes on your list. Now address them as the chair. Explain the problem in a few sentences. For example: 'If I listen to all of you, I won't pass this year and that is something I don't want.'

Then work out an action plan. Decide which wishes will be considered in which order and when, complete with priorities and agreements. For example: 'When I am studying, I don't want to be disturbed' or 'If one of you has an urgent problem, obey me when I tell you when you can return and I promise I'll be there.'

Thank the guests and say goodbye.

When you feel your concentration slipping while studying because you want to do other things or you are bored (i.e., the participants of the meeting in the Knight's hall have returned), then remind everyone of the agreements and act accordingly.

Note: You will have noticed from the answers to the questions 'What is your intention? What do you ultimately want to achieve?' that all intentions were good. Even those of the wishes that are disruptive. Only the form is inconvenient or ineffective for studying. It is important to be aware of this. And, of course, this makes sense because all wishes are products of your own mind. This means only the form and the timing need to be managed. Luckily, this is something that can be done.

8.3 Active learning methods

There is something else you can do to improve your concentration. You can invest in active learning methods. This may sound odd. After all, is there such a thing as inactive learning? Yes, there is. For example, when you re-read the material and underline a sentence here and there. Of course, you are not completely inactive when you do this, but there are methods that are much more active and constructive. And, therefore, more effective. Take, for instance, one of the methods described below.

Quiz yourself

Make a list of questions that you expect to get during the exam. Copy them onto memory cards. (The cards can be paper or digital.) Write the question on the front and the answer on the back of each card. You can also use the questions at the end of the chapter or on the study book's website for this purpose. Place the cards in a big bowl. Pull a card out regularly and take the time to answer the question. If you don't know the answer, look it up immediately.

Short, regular tests are the most effective. Do you need to go to the bathroom? Then take a few cards with you.

Research has shown that frequent repetition helps initiate the formation of memory paths. This will make it easier for you to come up with the right answer during the exam.

Explain the material out loud

Close your book or laptop, turn around and pretend to explain what you have just read or studied to your (imaginary) nine-year-old niece. Explain the material in 30 seconds after each

20-minute study block, in one minute after each hour of studying, in seven minutes at the end of each day, and in 30 minutes at the end of the week. Every time you fail to do so, look up the answer in your book and explain it to your 'niece'. Be prepared to answer any imaginary questions she throws at you.

Prepare for reading

When you need to read a chapter, paragraph or a whole book, you can simply start at the beginning and continue until you have reached the end. Although this makes sense, it isn't the best way to approach your reading assignment. There are some special techniques you can use to prepare your mind for reading. This will help you to read faster and remember what you have read better. You prepare a track, as it were, in your brain by marking the finish and laying out a trail. Once you have done this, you can actually start reading.

> You prepare a track, as it were, in your brain by marking the finish and laying out a trail

First, read the conclusion or the end of the text. This way, your brain knows the direction in which you will be heading. Then read the table of contents or the titles of the paragraphs. This will give your brain an idea of the framework of the text, so when you start reading the words and sentences will be placed in an existing structure. This means you won't have to do two things at once: read and structure the text.

One last thing before you get started: scan the text diagonally before giving it a proper read. By this I mean peruse the text from the top left to the bottom right in a zigzag pattern, so that you know what to expect.

9 OVERCOMING PROCRASTINATION

Procrastination is special kind of inattention. Students who procrastinate often say things like:
- 'I have already prepared this several times, so I'll be fine.'
- 'I'll get around to it tomorrow.'
- 'Planning is just not my thing.'
- 'Every time there's something else that is keeping me from starting.'
- 'Great, I'm on my way!'
- 'What's all the fuss?'
- 'There are other things that are important in life, too.'
- 'Nobody tells me what to do or when to do it.'

This may sound like someone with a relaxed, independent and easy-going attitude. And yes, procrastinating also has its advantages. If cleaning is your way of procrastinating, your house will be spotless. Or if seeing friends is your way of procrastinating, it will definitely boost your social life. But it can also make your life difficult. Work will pile up, your friends will get angry or you won't achieve the study goals you have set for yourself.

9.1 Different types of procrastinators

There are various types of procrastinators.
- The optimist. This type of procrastinator is happy and doesn't have a care in the world. Optimists tend to say things like, 'What are you worried about? Enjoy life. Things will work out.' Their cup is always half full. But in the end, they don't get the job done. And although it may seem as if this doesn't bother them, their procrastination can also be a way of pretending to be tougher than they are.
- The intimidated. This type of student is insecure and afraid of failing. Afraid of not being perfect, of being criticised or not being smart enough (see Chapter 5, Fixed mindset). They are also less capable of dealing with stress.
- The overloaded. This type of student wants or has to do too much. They may need to take care of family members alongside their studies. They may play sports at top level. Or work too hard. They are always busy and, whether they want or not, have to postpone things in order to manage.

9.2 Reasons for procrastination

When it comes to specific reasons why people procrastinate, the following are among the most common.
- Procrastination has become a habit.
- The expectation of success is low or too low.
- The expected reward is low or too low.
- Version 1: you are afraid due to fear of failure.
- Version 2: you are afraid due to perfectionism.
- You feel overwhelmed.

The first possible reason for procrastination is that your behaviour has become a habit. You have never gotten into trouble because of it and have gotten away with it. Or there was some sort of pay-off, like more time to spend on fun activities.

A second logical reason is that you don't believe your chance of success is very high. Perhaps your self-confidence is low, your study schedule is too full or you're not making enough of an effort. If you don't think it is very likely that you will succeed, then what is the point of doing your best?

Or you may procrastinate because the reward is not attractive enough or won't come soon enough. If there is a choice between short-term rewards and long-term rewards, most people tend to go for instant gratification. Long-term goals are generally the result of a rational process in your mind. In psychology, this is called 'cold cognition', the processing of information independently of emotional involvement. It manifests in not being easily irritated, thinking first, considering the consequences, being cautious and contemplating the long-term advantages and disadvantages. Short-term goals are about what you want to accomplish today. They almost always concern emotion, feeling, being in the here and now. You see your friends (feels good!), you play a few more levels of a game (feels good!) or you clean up (feels good!). Psychologists call this 'hot cognition'. Your emotional state influences your decision-making which is why, in this case, you prefer to immediately respond to the potential reward. In practice, hot (feeling) tends to win over cold (reasoning). How do you link hot short-term goals to cold long-term goals? By boosting your motivation. You can read more about this in Chapter 10.

> **Short-term goals are about what you want to accomplish today**

Now let's talk about fear, a familiar feeling among most procrastinators. Are you afraid of putting in the effort, only to come up short? Then it makes sense to procrastinate. Because if you fail your test or exam, you can always say, 'See, I was right. I'm no good at this' or 'If I had started studying sooner, I would have passed.'

Perfectionists base their self-worth on how they perform, on being successful. They don't want to make mistakes because this makes them less valuable as persons. So, the habit of procrastination or avoidance feels natural. Perfectionists often equate being evaluated with being judged. When they procrastinate, they postpone the moment of being judged, and possibly, rejected. It's irrational, but to them it feels very real all the same. There is also a big disadvantage: they are turning away from the opportunity to learn and grow. Is fear of failure or perfectionism something you struggle with? If you would like to learn more about these topics, then read *From Stress to Success*.

> Perfectionists often equate being evaluated with being judged

Now let's talk about feeling overwhelmed. It is very common for students to feel overwhelmed with university life. They look at what they have to do, whether it's a course or specific topic they have to master, a book they have to read or an assignment they need to do, and they get so overwhelmed that they are unable to function. So much so, they can't get started. It's too much to handle. They haven't got a clue where to start. Here's a tip. Divide up tasks into smaller ones if you feel overwhelmed. Then group these smaller chunks according to theme. Reserve time to study or tackle these chunks, group by group.

9.3 An exercise in reducing procrastination

Resisting procrastination often doesn't work. Nor does thinking of yourself as stupid or lazy. Nor ignoring or willing away the urge to procrastinate. Something inside you wants your attention. It's true that the form, the act of procrastinating, is inconvenient. But what would happen if you allowed that part of you to exist? If you would bend like bamboo? This is the purpose of the next exercise, which has proven to be very effective.

Exercise — Bamboo

Calling yourself stupid or getting angry at yourself doesn't make sense, and more importantly, it doesn't make your life any better. It's a waste of energy. Going with the flow is a better idea in this case. Think of bamboo!

Follow these steps:
1. Have a stopwatch (or the timer on your mobile phone) ready while you study.
2. Make an agreement with yourself that as soon as your attention starts to wander, an internal alarm will go off. (Beware that sometimes your mind can wander for a while without you noticing.)
3. When you tune out, set the timer for five minutes. Stand up or push your study material aside. Do something completely different, and make sure you enjoy it thoroughly.
4. When the five minutes are over, start studying again with all your attention.
5. Repeat the above when you find yourself wandering. And again, and again, if necessary.

After a while you will notice that you can work more calmly and for longer periods at a time.

9.4 More tips

Whatever kind of procrastinator you are, whatever your reasons are, if you want to procrastinate less, here are a few tips that can help.

- Don't let being overwhelmed paralyse you. Breaking up large tasks into manageable chunks can help you get moving on those scary priorities you've been putting off.
- Do half of the task. Or a third, or a quarter. Be kind to yourself. If you should cover 20 pages, then do 10. If you planned to work for two hours, work for one hour.
- Do the unpleasant bits first ('Eat the frog first' as the Americans say).
- Reward yourself regularly, even when finishing small chunks.
- Do the task or activity, even if you don't feel like it.
- Come up with three reasons why it makes sense to start studying. Or ask a housemate. An outsider often has a fresh perspective on things.
- Establish a routine to work in blocks with a fixed length. Reserve set periods in the week for studying. The more routine and regularity, the less space there is for 'negotiation'. Well-trodden paths are easier to stick to.
- If rewards work better for you than punishment, think of a good reward for when you complete a certain task. Incorporate smaller rewards throughout studying. If you are more sensitive to punishment, then think of something you would hate. For example, 'If I don't complete this task by Friday, I can't go out on Saturday night'.
- Give yourself a boost. Once the engine is running, it will keep going. Really make an effort. When you think, 'I don't

want to', simply take a deep breath, smile and turn this thought around into something positive, like 'Boy, do I want to get this done! I'm going to make a cup of tea and roll up my sleeves. I'm in the mood for studying!' And then literally jump up to get started.

- Plan a study date with a friend. Meet in the library and take a break once an hour. This will keep both of you focussed while having fun.
- Give yourself a kick up the backside. Or arrange for someone else to give you one.

10 MOTIVATION: HOW DO YOU KEEP IT UP?

Does 'I'm no longer motivated' sound like something you could say? Do you also see that you may mean different things? There are various forms of motivation. If you are having study problems, it is important to know what kind of motivation issues you are having. The more insight you have into the underlying issue, the better you will be able to determine what you need to solve the problem.

10.1 Short-term vs long-term motivation

Find out if you are having short-term or long-term motivation issues. Not feeling like studying today (short-term motivation issue) and having second thoughts about your studies (long-term motivation issue) are two entirely different things. Motivation for the medium term could refer to, for example, finishing the year.

Unfortunately, the different durations – short term, medium term and long term – do not stimulate each other automatically. Even if you really want to become a lawyer (long-term goal), this doesn't mean you will find enough motivation to prepare for the exam or the test scheduled for next week (short term). Conversely, you may be highly motivated to pass an exam, but have no idea what you will do once you graduate. In Chapter 9, you read that most people prefer instant gratification over delayed gratification. The same applies to motivation. It is more difficult to muster motivation for long-term goals than short-term goals.

Would you like to improve your motivation quickly? Be creative and find ways to incorporate short-term rewards for yourself.

Tips:
- Treat yourself to a nice cup of coffee early in the morning when you are having difficulty getting out of bed.
- Go to the cinema after every exam you have passed.
- After you pass four exams, treat yourself to a city trip, festival or an entire Sunday of binge watching your favourite TV show.
- Highlight all the parts of your plan that you have completed with a yellow marker. Doesn't that feel great? The more sections you highlight, the more eager you will become. Note: If you do not manage to complete many parts of your plan, then highlighting can have a negative effect and make you feel worse. In this case, it is best to stop and prepare a new, more realistic plan.

10.2 Are you really motivated, or are you doing it because you are supposed to do it?

Are you having long-term motivation issues? Are you having second thoughts about your studies? Are you unsure whether you will like the career you are preparing for? In this case, it is important to know whether the choice you have made is truly yours. Do you want to do this course for yourself or are you doing it to please, for instance, your parents? It is not necessarily a bad thing to do something for someone else, but it can affect your motivation. When you are intrinsically motivated, you will find it more enjoyable and easier to persevere when things get tough.

If you have chosen this course to make someone else happy and you are struggling, then you have several options. You can drop out. This can be a smart thing to do if you are miserable. You can talk about it. Coming clean to your parents may seem daunting, but usually works out well. How can they know what you are feeling if you don't put your cards on the table? Perhaps they won't even want you to continue if it is making you unhappy.

> Coming clean to your parents may seem daunting, but usually works out well

You could also continue studying and think of something that does motivate you and will cause you to take action. For example, 'I want to experience how it feels to finish something that I have started'.

10.3. More causes of reduced motivation (and possible solutions)

Take a look at the table below. It may contain tips that could help you improve your motivation.

My motivation is dwindling because...	Possible solutions
... other people demand too much of me.	<ul><li>Learn to stand up for yourself.</li><li>Create a risk analysis: will the world come to an end if you say 'no'?</li><li>Work on your self-confidence.</li><li>Ask others for advice when making your planning.</li></ul>
... I don't know why I'm doing what I am doing.	<ul><li>Revisit your motives for taking this course.</li><li>Be honest with yourself. Is your lack of motivation caused by not wanting to do it? Or are you having problems and therefore less able to do it?</li></ul>
... I just can't seem to get around to doing what I need to do.	Do something about your procrastination. It pays to spend more time studying. Mastering something is fun and stimulates learning even more about it!
... I just don't feel like doing it anymore.	Motivation is much more than feeling like doing something. You are motivated because you expect something to be interesting, challenging and pleasant. Or because you believe it will benefit you in some way. If you are truly motivated, you can move mountains. Even if you don't feel like it sometimes. Create short-term goals and rewards in addition to long-term goals and rewards.

My motivation is dwindling because...	Possible solutions
... the study material is too difficult or there are too many difficult words in the text.	To understand a text, you do not have to understand all of the words. Difficult words can make you doubt your ability to understand something and undermine your self-confidence. However, they are not necessarily relevant for understanding the text as a whole. Underline the difficult words, copy them and look them up. Check which words are useful for your course. Make a glossary of these words. You can forget about the other difficult words.
... the study material is too unclear.	Create a mind map (see Chapter 11).
... I keep getting distracted.	<ul><li>Study for shorter periods of time.</li><li>Make sure the place where you are studying is quiet.</li><li>Read Chapter 8, Concentrating.</li></ul>
... I'm afraid of what others will think of me if I fail.	<ul><li>Set realistic and feasible goals.</li><li>Work on a growth mindset.</li><li>If you are really struggling, go see a Student Psychologist. A Student Psychologist can help you become less dependent on what others think of you.</li></ul>

My motivation is dwindling because…	Possible solutions
… I just can't do it.	Analyse what it is exactly that you can't do. You made it this far, so you must be doing something right! What is going well and what could be improved? For example, distinguishing between main and secondary issues, making and sticking to a plan, setting priorities, taking good notes, speed reading, cramming, or processing a lot of material in a short amount of time. Try new strategies, evaluate them and see what could be improved. See whether your faculty or university offers courses to train specific study skills.

10.4 You don't have to feel like it to do it

'I don't care if you don't feel like it. Just do it!' Does this sound like your parents? They may be annoying, but they have a point. If you study properly, you can get good grades even if you don't really like what you do. It all boils down to self-discipline, the willpower to resist temptations, and perseverance and self-control. Although motivation is a huge factor in successful learning, it's not the dealbreaker. What's more, motivation does not increase with increased performance. Sometimes, the first step to becoming more motivated is to muster all the self-discipline you've got and just get started.

11 MIND MAPS

You have done everything to prepare for studying. You have made a plan. If your plan was too ambitious, you cut it down to a more manageable size. You found smart ways to focus and to avoid procrastination. Now it's time for the next stage of the Circle of Learning Success. It's time to establish brain circuits.

Mind mapping is an important tool that can help you with this. It requires some effort, but the rewards are great and worthwhile. Mind mapping is a special technique for taking notes that makes it easier for students to remember and recall information.

> It's time to establish brain circuits

Mind maps are diagrams that visually link a central subject or concept to related concepts, ideas or tasks, which are represented by single words or images (or both). Mind mapping is a technique that helps you use both sides of your brain, mixing images, forms and colours with language, logic and structure. This enhances your brain's capacity.

11.1 The cons of common note-taking methods

Most students take notes by copying entire sentences or the main points as they encounter them. Is this the most effective way to take notes? No, definitely not. Here's why.

- It isn't clear how the different points connect with one another.
- You don't rank the different elements that you write down.
- By copying entire sentences, your brain switches to slumber mode because it thinks it has all the information it needs.

As said earlier, everything in the brain revolves around making connections. This requires logic and structure. Without this, the connections are incoherent and basically useless.

Mind maps use the brain's talent to make associations, and to rank and add information. And also, the brain's ability for visual recognition.

Association

When information enters the brain, it seeks to find existing patterns, areas where it has prior knowledge. The brain opens each drawer and rifles through the contents, as it were, asking itself, 'Have I seen this before? Where does this belong? Where do I store this? How is it connected to previous information?'. If the brain can't associate it with anything, the new information is likely to be forgotten. Put otherwise, the more drawers the new information can be stored in, the easier it will be to remember.

Ranking

The brain can remember information more easily and recall information faster if it knows what information is very important, or less important. Ranking serves as a framework for structuring the access to information.

Sometimes study material lacks a clear structure, and it takes effort to categorise the text into manageable sections. You need to read closely to determine where to put the information in the mind map and what information is the most important. The central idea is the starting point of your mind map. This should be in the centre of your page. When you are actively thinking about this, the information becomes more deeply ingrained. The visual representation of the information on a mind map will also improve your ability to recall it.

Adding

A third important characteristic of the brain is that it tends to complete things when part of the information is missing. For example, if I sing: 'Happy birthday…', you'll sing 'to you' before you even realise it. This also applies to information that you don't know yet. The brain fills in missing information to compensate for the incomplete data. If you are on a train and the person next to you is talking on the phone and you hear part of the conversation, your brain will immediately try to fill in the blanks. It will try to guess what the person on the other end of the line is saying. It is nearly impossible to suppress this tendency.

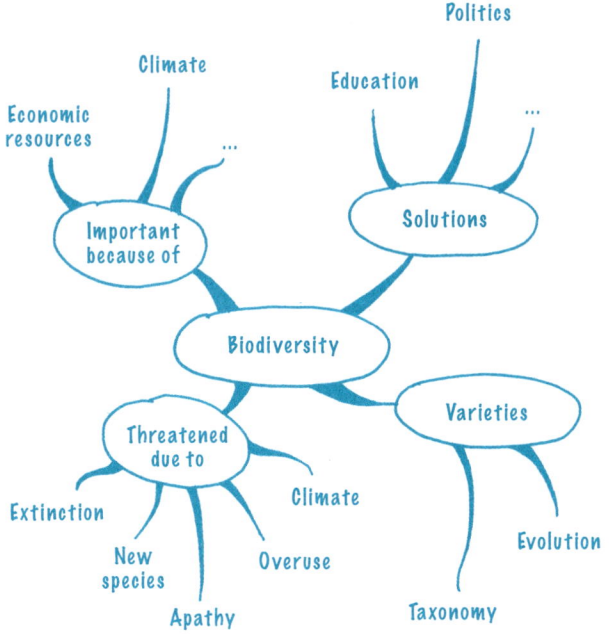

You can make use of your brain's natural inclination to add missing information by using key words. Key words are the main words in a sentence of paragraph. They draw your attention. You can find key words in the text, or you can make up your own when you summarise the text. Using key words helps keep the brain active. It's like setting the brain to a fill-in-the-blank mode, so it stays awake. When you read or hear the key word, your brain will automatically start to search for the missing information.

The power of images

'A picture says more than a thousand words' is a well-known saying. The brain is able, more or less, to store an unlimited number of images. It can perceive and remember images extremely quickly and precisely.

When you look at a mind map, which is essentially a visual diagram made up of colours, codes, pictures, symbols and lines, it's as if your brain takes a picture of it. It's super powerful. This does not work as well with a list of words or a long summary.

Some people say, 'Mind maps are not for me because I can't draw' or 'I can't think of anything'. Or they are considered childish and thus foolish. However, what is so great about mind maps is that you don't need to be good at drawing. What's more, practice makes perfect. There are many geniuses who used drawings to visualise and structure their ideas (see *The Mind Map Book* by Tony and Barry Buzan).

11.2 How do you go about it?

If you have never created a mind map before, there are plenty of tutorials online that will guide you through the basics. To get started, take a piece of paper and turn it landscape. Start in the centre of the page. The image or word in the centre represents the main theme or topic of the mind map. Write words that are related to the main theme on thick branches radiating out from the central theme. Add as many main theme branches around the map as you can think of. Now add branches linked to the main branch that triggered them. Add an image to all the branches to represent each word. You can use any symbol to visualise important words on your map – the quirkier, the better.

Start with a trial round. Use this round to determine:
- Your central theme or topic.
- The key words related to your main theme.
- The symbols you can use to visualise the key words.

> **Tips:**
> - Use simple shapes like ovals or rounded rectangles to represent the central ideas.
> - Use key words, not whole sentences.
> - Arrange all the elements intuitively. This will make it easier for you to remember.
> - Use block letters for words (rather than cursive) to facilitate reading.
> - Use as many images or symbols as possible.
> - Use as many different colours as possible.
> - Connect all the encircled words and images with one another.
> - Use as many different connection lines as possible: arrows, straight lines, curved lines, dotted lines, etc.
> - Add codes and abbreviations.

Be creative. Take the time to discover your own style. You can also start with a sketch, let it rest for a while, and return later to finalise it. You can, of course, adjust your mind map as often as you need based on new insights or perspectives, or to include new information.

11.3 To conclude

You can do mind maps on the computer, but they can also be hand-drawn. If you want to do yours digitally, there is mind mapping software available for nearly every digital platform. Simply go online and search 'best free mind mapping software'. It is also possible to download commercial software for trial periods. Of course, you can combine digital and hand-drawn elements by doing the broad outline on the computer, printing it, and then adding hand-drawn pictures, connection lines, codes and colours.

It's OK if your mind map is a bit messy. In fact, you should resist the urge to make it too neat and have everything perfectly lined up, because this will make it harder for you to remember it. So, get messy and have fun! As long as your mind map is legible and logical, that's all that matters.

Remember, mind mapping is a skill that takes a bit of practice. Don't expect to master it the first time you try it. First, give it a try, then refine it. If you get stuck, which very well may happen, then take a few deep breaths. After doing a few mind maps, you will notice that it will become easier. In time you will even develop your own style. As with any challenge, if you push through the first phase it will become second nature and you will reap the benefits for the rest of your life.

> **Remember, mind mapping is a skill that takes a bit of practice**

12 MNEMONICS: TRICKS FOR TRAINING YOUR MEMORY

Another way to remember things faster and more easily is by using memory techniques, or mnemonics. These techniques are clever to use if you need to remember lots of words or terms, or difficult terms. If you use memory tricks, you won't need any notes for a presentation, even if it is a long one.

The brain loves stories, images and novelties, especially things that deviate from the norm. As shown earlier, mind maps take advantage of this. The same goes for memory techniques. Most mnemonics unlock the brain's superpowers: story, image, association and emotion. The more superpowers the technique uses, the better it will work. Therefore, memory techniques focus on:

- Inventing images for the information you have to remember (as said earlier, it is a lot easier to remember images than words).
- Weaving loose elements into a story.
- Inserting emotional, new or funny elements in the images and stories.

> **Tips:**
> - Take your time.
> - Visualise what you want to remember.
> - Make it absurd. The more absurd the images and stories, the longer you will remember them.
> - Make use of emotions. The more emotions you incorporate, the better.
> - Create your own story by connecting images and emotions.

12.1 Use acronyms

Acronyms are a widely used memory technique. If you can turn the first letters of the words you want to remember into a new word, you are lucky. Take, for example, the four economic production factors of Capital, Entrepreneurship, Labour and Land. **CELL**!

If there are many words, you can use the first letters to make a new sentence. In physics, there are the colour codes for resistance: **B**lack – **B**rown – **R**ed – **O**range – **Y**ellow – **G**reen – **B**lue – **V**iolet – **G**rey – **W**hite. An acronym to remember this code is: Better Be Ready Or Your Great Big Venture Goes West. Another example: **T**era - **G**iga – **M**ega – **K**ilo – **M**illi – **M**icro – **N**ano – **P**ico can be remembered like: Tiny Green Mad Keys Measure Mainly Necessary People.

12.2 Take a stroll: the Loci method

About 2,500 years ago, a dining hall roof collapsed. Almost all the guests died under the rubble. The victims were horribly disfigured but fortunately, one of the survivors could remember exactly who all the deceased persons were. This survivor was the well-known poet Simonides, who used a memory technique that he invented himself called the Loci method.

This is how it works. You go on an imaginary journey in your mind. During this journey, or walk, you pass several landmarks ('loci' is the Latin word for 'location'). You link the words or numbers you must remember to these landmarks. Then you construct a story around these landmarks. You will not remember the individual words or numbers later, but you will remember the walk and the story associated with it. This will allow you to recall what you had to remember.

> You link the words or numbers you must remember to these landmarks

These are the steps to follow:
- Choose a familiar route. This could be in your own room or through the town where you live. Pick a different walk for each list or presentation you need to remember.
- Choose fixed landmarks along the route. Link those landmarks to the things you have to remember through associations. Make sure that the connections and associations mean something to you, however absurd they may be.
- Run through this route in your mind a few times, always in the same order, past the same landmarks.

Take, for example, a shopping list with the following items: bananas, yoghurt, toilet paper, potato chips, apple juice, beer. Start at the front door. In your mind you see a group of wild monkeys engaged in a fierce fight over bananas at the front door. You trip over a crushed banana on the floor and have to duck to avoid one sailing past your head. Bananas.

Once inside, you see white yoghurt dripping from the ceiling in the hallway. A few drops fall on your head. Yoghurt.

When you get to the door of your room, you see that your housemates have once again had fun sealing off the door with toilet paper. You go inside and put some toilet paper in your pocket. This will come in handy later. Toilet paper.

Once inside, you hear crunching sounds under your feet: the red carpet is covered with potato chips from last night's party. Potato chips.

On your left, your naked and exhausted girlfriend is lying on the bed. Eve, the first woman on earth. Eve and the apple. Apple juice.

You sit on the edge of the bed. But then you jump because it is not your girlfriend lying on your bed. There is only one way to deal with that, and that is to have a beer. Luckily, there is a beer tap above your pillow. Beer.

Once you have done this walk three times in your mind, you will be able to recall everything in the supermarket without a shopping list. And next week you will still remember it if you shut your eyes for a moment and picture the walk.

12.3 You don't have to be a brilliant storyteller

You don't have to be a storyteller or a highly creative person to use this technique. We can all come up with a route if we take the time to sit down and do it. The more you see, feel, experience and smell, the better you will remember. This applies to all memory techniques; they all focus on associations. What does the word make you think of? What is the first thing that comes to mind? Think of something that appeals to you. And remember:

- The more absurd, colourful and lively the association, the easier it will be to remember.
- The more often you practise, the faster and better you will get at it.

13 EXAMS: TRAINING FOR DIFFERENT TYPES OF EXAMS

The previous chapters were mainly about you as a person. We talked about how your brain works, how powerful your thoughts are (or can be), and how to deal with procrastination and increase your motivation. Now it's time for the next topic: taking exams.

There are different types of exams and each has different requirements. Some types may suit you better than others. It's like with people, some you like, some you don't. But it makes sense to try and get along anyway. So, instead of getting worked up, it would be better to find out how to best deal with that annoying neighbour of yours and to use this knowledge to your advantage. Similarly, every type of exam has a set of rules. If you are aware of them, you will be much better prepared when you take the exam.

> There are different types of exams and each has different requirements. Some types may suit you better than others

This chapter discusses the rules for multiple-choice exams and open-book exams. You can find more information online about these and other types of exams.

> What is the best way to practise your exam skills?
>
> Practise taking an exam!

13.1 Multiple-choice exams

It is certainly not the case that you don't have to study as hard for a multiple-choice exam, that you can pass them with just a few tricks, or that they only test factual knowledge. The same preconditions apply to multiple-choice exams as to other types of tests:

- Know what is expected of you. Review the module's learning objectives and do half of all the practice exams to check whether the learning objectives are being tested in the way you expect.
- Make sure that you can explain the study material out loud to someone else. This is a sign that the necessary brain networks are strong enough and the information is properly ingrained.
- Make sure that you are well rested and comfortable.

Now let's move on to the multiple-choice exam itself. The four techniques described below will allow you to make more and better use of the networks you have already established in your brain. This will ensure better results and increase your chances of passing the exam.

1. Complete the exam in three rounds

At the start of the exam, your brain has its highest levels of oxygen and nutrition (glucose). This is when it functions at its best. It's smart to make use of that. In the first round, answer all questions that you know off the top of your head. It would be a pity if you wait and get these questions wrong because you are too tired to think straight. In the second round, you tackle the questions that are a bit more difficult. The last round is for the most difficult ones. This method will give you more time to concentrate on the questions that require more time. And if you run out of time, you will at least have answered the easy questions correctly.

2. Cover the answers

Rephrase the question as if it were an open question. Work out the answer on a separate piece of paper.

Suppose you get this exam question:
Economic scarcity is when:
a. the resources exceed the possibilities;
b. there are insufficient resources in relation to the needs;
c. there is insufficient need for a particular good in relation to resources;
d. there are sufficient resources to meet the needs.

The key words are 'economy – scarcity – resources – needs – a good'. If you let your brain go to work, it will scan all five key words looking for links and connections. This takes a great deal of unnecessary time and energy. After all, you don't want recognition or random associations, you want an answer to the question.

Cover the answers. Turn the question into an open question. For example: 'How is economic scarcity defined?'. Your brain can now calmly look for the answer more quickly. Work out the answer on a separate piece of paper if you find the question difficult (second or third round). If your grade is lower than you would like it to be, this will give you important information that you can use to improve yourself.

> **If you let your brain go to work, it will scan all five key words looking for links and connections**

Do not look at the four multiple-choice answers before you have answered the open question. Uncover the answers. Which answer resembles the answer you came up with most?

Note: If you are not allowed to use blank paper during an exam to work out answers, ask the student representatives to submit an official request to do so. Not being allowed scrap paper violates the basic right that students have when taking an exam.

3. Insert answers in the question

What if your answer does not immediately lead to a hit when you look at the possible multiple-choice answers? In most cases, two answers jump out at you as obviously incorrect. Discard those. Insert the two remaining answers in the question and see which one makes the most sense. Economic scarcity is when… [answer 1]. Or: Economic scarcity is when… [answer 2].

If this doesn't help, try a different approach. If you're not sure on a conscious level, then think about the question on a subconscious level. How certain are you on a scale from 1 to 100 that the first option is true? What about option 2? Go with the first answer that pops into your mind! Suppose you arrive at 79 and 81. Then your doubts are understandable as the numbers are very close together. You are right to hesitate. But 81 is higher than 79, so go for the option that goes with 81.

4. Only change your answers based on reflection and a changed perspective

In all cases, you should only change your answers if you have thought about them and have changed your perspective. Make a note of this during your exam. For each question, write down how certain you are of your answer on a scale from 1 to 5, with 5 being '100% certain'. Also highlight any questions that you ended up changing. You will need that information later for the analysis. If you changed your answer, ask yourself these two questions:

- How certain were you of your first answer?
- Did you change your answer for the better?

If you incorrectly changed all the answers to questions that you were 100% sure of then the solution is very simple: next time, don't do it! If you were right to change most questions, then it's a good idea to keep doing that.

13.2 Open-book exams

The best way to prepare for open-book exams is to read your study books thoroughly. It is very bad practice not to read the main material and only rely on summaries. The skills tested in this type of exam include:
- Distinguishing between main and secondary information.
- Being able to formulate answers clearly, briefly and concisely (writing skill).
- Finding relevant information quickly. (Do you know where to look? Are you good at seeing connections and does this help you to narrow down your search?)

> **Tips:**
> - Buy all study books (new or second-hand).
> - Read them, too!
> - Make notes in your book and mark important passages.
> - Turn down the corners of important pages or use sticky notes so you can find them more easily.

A book should be leafed through from front to back, and opened and shut frequently. The more well-thumbed a book is, the more information you will have retained. Some students don't want to spoil their books by writing in them. Hopefully, you will be able to get past this. There are professionals who say that years later they can still see the page with the highlighted or underlined answer they are looking for. Sometimes this produces the answer immediately. In any case, it is a very efficient method for finding things: you know exactly where you need to be.

There are two fundamental rules for marking a text:

1. Mark the text after reading the entire chapter or section. This way, you have a clearer idea of the essence of the text.
2. Do not mark more than 15 to 20% of a page. If you mark more, this means you could have trouble distinguishing between the main and secondary issues. Double-check if what you have highlighted is correct by comparing notes with a student, teacher or mentor. If you haven't got it right, make sure that you get better at it by practising or taking a course on this topic. Sometimes it is unavoidable that a page is full of highlighted lines because the text is dense with relevant information. In this case, highlighting won't be very helpful. Try using another method, such as mind mapping.

14 TAKING EXAMS: THRIVING ON THE RIGHT AMOUNT OF STRESS

All right. You are familiar with the type of exam and have studied attentively. You completely understand the material and have reviewed or applied it. All the necessary networks have been established and strengthened. You feel ready for the exam. Bring it on!

The trick is to ensure that everything that is in your head comes out during the exam. The most important aspect in this respect is to make sure you're in good shape. Not just physically, but also mentally and emotionally. This means that your heart and mind should be clear of worries or unpleasant thoughts. There is a lot you can do in advance: you can make sure you are relaxed, you can practise a growth mindset, or you can discuss your study issues with someone from your faculty.

However, no matter how well prepared you are, you can still draw a blank during an exam. If this happens to you, it helps to have an emergency relaxation plan in place. Are you the type of student who needs stress to perform well? As with everything in life, balance is key. You shouldn't be too tense, but not too relaxed either.

14.1 Is it better to relax or increase your focus before an exam?

If you suffer from test anxiety, it is important to get plenty of rest the day before your exam or presentation. Cramming at the last minute, trying to cover every morsel of information you may have missed, is the last thing you should do. This can cause existing information to be overwritten, which means you are doing more harm than good. You might want to lightly read over your notes for the next day, but nothing more than that. Top athletes don't do any sprinting or extensive training before an important competition either. Instead, they relax. So, go to the sauna, take a walk or do something else that relaxes you.

On the other hand, some students need pressure to help keep them focussed. If you don't feel any pressure at all, try giving yourself a pep talk. Tell yourself why you want to pass this exam or give a good presentation. In this case, reviewing the material before the exam or presentation can be useful.

14.2 Tips for taking exams

- Make sure you are wearing your best clothes and underwear (seriously!). This also works for job interviews by the way.
- Take something to eat and drink with you, preferably something low in sugar. Quick-sugar foods give you an initial boost of energy, but their after-effects make you feel sleepy. So have a banana rather than a bar of chocolate.
- Make sure you have plenty of scrap paper, two pens, two pencils and an eraser.

- Steer clear of students who quiz each other or do some last-minute revising. All this does is release stress hormones, and stress makes it more difficult to recall stored information. The chance that precisely these questions will come up in the exam is very small anyway.

14.3 Four exercises for when you draw a blank

If you notice during the exam that stress is getting the better of you and you're drawing a blank, you need to take care of that first. Your body is too upset to answer questions properly. Your breathing is rapid and shallow, you begin to sweat, your body's hot-cold balance is disrupted, and you're plagued by crippling thoughts ('Oh no, here we go again', 'I don't remember anything', 'I can't do this'). Remember that your way of reacting is caused by something in your past, even if you are not aware of it. A process has preceded this situation and that process can be reversed.

Exercise – You are the boss
Test anxiety is the perfect breeding ground for undermining thoughts. When your stress levels rise those negative thoughts are having a ball. *Fiesta fiesta, baila baila*. Did you give them permission to party? Remember that you are the boss, you determine what thoughts are allowed to swirl in your mind and body. And if a thought isn't helpful, swap it out.

Here's what to do. Sit properly with your legs side by side, your back firmly against the chair and your hands resting comfortably on your lap. Close your eyes and take a few deep breaths. Replace your negative thoughts with these thoughts:
- 'Nobody is dying and nothing is on fire.'
- 'These negative thoughts are not helping me. I'm putting an end to this drama.'
- 'I also passed the last exam, despite being stressed.'
- 'Teachers want their students to pass their course.'
- 'I don't need self-confidence to pass an exam. I just need to be prepared.' (Research has shown this to be true.)

- 'I'm well prepared. The answers are all in my head.'
- 'The stress that I'm feeling provides a better flow of oxygen to my brain. This is a good thing. I'm going to use that extra oxygen.'

You can also choose a mantra that works for you. Repeat it silently until you are ready to return to the exam question and are able to focus and use your knowledge to answer it. Continue to inhale deeply while repeating the mantra if this is helpful.

Exercise – A pleasant, warm light
The second exercise goes like this. Visualise the location of the crippling thoughts in your forehead. Take a deep breath. Exhale slowly. Notice how these stressful thoughts sink down towards your heart with every exhalation. Let your shoulders sink along with them. When the thoughts reach your heart, they are absorbed one by one in a large, pleasant, warm light. See the bright light and feel the warmth. Feel the thoughts dissolve. Do this several times, like a soft stroking movement downwards from your head across your face to your neck, your chest and finally your heart. Keep going until your forehead is empty and all stressful thoughts have melted into the great warm light of your heart. Then move your head and shoulders, stretch your back and sigh deeply several times.

Exercise – Breathe and relax 1

The third exercise is a breathing exercise. Some students think breathing exercises are too woolly to be helpful, but I assure you this isn't true. Breathing regulates the neurophysiological processes in our brains, including our stress responses. This is hardcore science, there's nothing woolly about it.

Sit properly with your legs next to each other, your back firmly against the chair and your hands resting comfortably on your lap. Close your eyes and take a few deep abdominal breaths. Each time you inhale, your belly should expand. As you exhale, your belly returns to a normal resting state. If your shoulders are pulled up toward your ears, relax and lower them.

Repeat the following sentence silently while you continue to breathe: 'I'm returning to the moment when I felt good and relaxed'. Feel how your consciousness is 'rewound' while you continue to breathe deeply. Notice how your heart rate slows, how your breathing sinks into your abdomen and how the sweating stops. Your mind is feeling increasingly empty, like a beautiful, peaceful and sunny beach. Imagine that you can smell the freshness of the water and hear the birds chirping.

Exercise – Breathe and relax 2

This last relaxation exercise may seem strange, but try it anyway. It really works! Here's how it goes:

- You should do this exercise in a sitting and grounded position, with your feet flat on the floor, your back and bottom firmly in the chair, your shoulders relaxed.
- Put the fingertips of your left and right hand against each other, pinkie to pinkie, ring finger to ring finger, and so on.
- Close your eyes and concentrate on your breathing. Continue to breathe calmly and rhythmically. Seek 'the lowest point' of your breathing.
- Press the fingertips of your pinkies and ring fingers against each other and interlock your other fingers. (Your hands should be in a half-prayer position.)
- Notice how your breathing sinks deeper as you do this. You can now breathe so deeply that you feel your pelvic floor moving with every breath you take.
- Release your pinkies and ring fingers. Press your two middle fingers against each other. The other fingers remain interlocked. Note that your breathing rises slightly.
- Now release your middle fingers and press your two index fingers against each other. You'll notice that your breathing rises further.

In other words, by bringing the two fingertips of different fingers together, you can bring your breathing up and down again. Do this exercise for several minutes. Focussing on your breathing in the lower part of your body will calm you down and help you to relax. As a result, you will be better able to concentrate on the exam questions.

If you know yourself well enough to anticipate freezing up during an exam or a presentation, practise using these exercises in advance when nothing is at stake. Soldiers also train before going into battle. This is done when there is no imminent danger. So, make sure you become familiar with the breathing techniques by bringing your breathing down to your abdomen several times a day and breathing more slowly and calmly. This can be done for periods as short as a few seconds or minutes. Also, a few times a day, check whether you are thinking helpful or unhealthy thoughts. If your thoughts aren't helpful, dismiss them and choose a different, more positive thought. This way, positive thoughts will become familiar, you can recall them more easily and they will be more effective when you draw a blank during an exam.

If the above doesn't work for you, you can always concentrate on an image of a kitten (or a tadpole or the Eiffel Tower, whatever works for you). Now hold that image in your mind. Hold it, hold it, hold it. Every second is beneficial and worth it, because it reduces the output of your brain's stress network.

It can also be helpful to look at things with a sense of humour. Take a step back and look at yourself. Use your imagination. How would Harry Potter, for example, deal with his boggart. This famous scene illustrates how laughing at your demons can be very powerful and make them disappear! Humour relaxes us. If you can laugh at the situation, this takes care of half of the problem.

15 THE PITFALLS OF A RESIT

It would be fantastic if the tips and insights in this book help you to get good grades. However, it is still possible that you fail an exam and that the resit turns out to be much more difficult than you expect. Not because you've become stupid all of a sudden. Of course not! There are other reasons, or pitfalls as we call them, for this. The next section focusses on the pitfalls of a resit.

> **It is still possible that you fail an exam and that the resit turns out to be much more difficult than you expect**

Tips for resitting exams:
- Trick yourself into thinking you are studying for the resit for the first time.
- If you retake the exam in the next academic year, check carefully to make sure your study materials and goals are still relevant.
- Exchange notes with a fellow student. This will give you a fresh perspective.

15.1 Pitfalls

Pitfall 1: negative feelings take over

> Not passing an exam or a test can trigger a stress response. Stress impairs your ability to concentrate and study. In turn, this creates a greater risk of failing again. This is called 'magical failing'.

Frustration increases the chance of failing again, as does insecurity. When we are frustrated, insecure or stressed out, certain neurochemicals are released in the brain that hinder the process of learning, remembering and reproducing information successfully.

A second effect is that negative feelings use up part of our working memory. The brain does this automatically to relieve itself of unpleasant feelings, such as frustration or stress. It needs space to deal with these feelings, and for this it uses part of the working memory. This means that part of your working memory becomes unavailable to you, which affects your ability to concentrate.

As said earlier, IQ is like the horsepower (HP) of a car. What good is it if you never take the car out of the garage? Success, whether in your studies or future career, depends to a great extent on how you use that HP. So, use your intelligence! Take a few deep breaths, stretch your body, put your negative feelings on hold, and get to work.

Pitfall 2: keep doing the same as you did before

Imagine seeing a doctor and telling him or her, 'Doctor, the pills don't work'. You hope that the doctor won't say, 'Never mind, just keep taking them'. Instead, you want to be taken seriously and examined properly.

This may seem obvious, but the same reasoning could be applied to resits. If something went wrong the first time, you should examine the reason for this. This means that if you failed an exam, it does not make sense to prepare for the resit in exactly the same way as for the exam ('Never mind, just keep taking them'). Something needs to be improved. And to improve something, you need to know what went wrong. Ask yourself the following questions:

- What type of questions did I get wrong? (Detailed questions or general questions?)
- Did I make mistakes at the beginning or at the end of the exam?
- Which topics were hard for me?
- Did I incorrectly change any answers?
- Did I make mistakes because I misread the question or wasn't accurate enough?
- Did I run out of time?

It helps if you can be objective and look at the exam as if it were someone else's. Pretend you have to tell 'the other person' in broad terms what you think went wrong and give him or her advice based on your findings.

When preparing for the resit, you don't have to pay as much attention to revising the parts that you did well on. Keep checking that you still know those parts though. If you can explain them out loud, they are still in your head. It goes without saying that the parts that you don't master are those that require more attention.

If you fail an exam by a small margin each time, it doesn't mean that you 'almost passed' each time. It means that you have not adequately mastered the material at all. You need to work on that.

Pitfall 3: recognising the material instead of really mastering it

A huge pitfall is thinking you have mastered the material because you have studied it a lot. If your brain could speak, you would hear it say, 'Yes, I recognise that, and that too'. However, there is a big difference between recognising and really knowing it!

It is fairly easy to check if you have fallen into the trap of recognition. If you start thinking, 'Yes, I know or recognise this', then close your book or notebook and explain out loud what you have just read. If you can, you have retained it. You have mastered the material. If you can't, you need to go over it again.

15.2 Approaching the study material in a different way

There are various ways to avoid the pitfalls of a resit. Several of them are listed above. Here are some more tips:
- Use other books and materials, too. For example, look for videos on the topic.

- Get a fellow student to ask you lots of questions.
- Explain the study material to a family member or friend who is not familiar with the topic. You will quickly find out if you've mastered the material. If you don't, you will struggle to put it into your own words and explain it to someone else.
- Use the tombola exercise below. It's a fun way to practise the material.

> **Exercise – The tombola**
> - Collect two or more old exams. Cut out the individual questions and fold them in two, like lottery tickets. Place them in a big bowl. Keep the answers out of sight on a separate piece of paper.
> - Take out a random question.
> - Read it carefully and take the time to think out loud what the answer should be.
> - Then look at the answer to see if you are right.
> - Is your answer correct? Then pick another question.
> - Did you get it wrong? Explain out loud why you thought your answer was correct. Look at the answer to the question and compare it with yours. Try to figure out where you went wrong. Was your reasoning incorrect, or did you link matters that did not belong together?
> - Then read the relevant study material again.

The advantage of this method is that you can use the answers, whether you got them right or wrong, to find out which sections you need to study more closely. In addition, it also leads to insight. Knowing why you did not get the right answer will help you to understand what the answer should be. The tombola is also a fun way of revising some key topics, for instance at the end of the day.

16 PERSEVERANCE

From waitress to congresswoman
Alexandria Ocasio-Cortez comes from a poor family in the Bronx. Her entire family saved up for her and her brother to continue their education. And successfully so. During her second year of college, Alexandria's father dies of lung cancer. After graduation, things do not become any easier. Alexandria struggles to find a job at her level of education. She turns to waitressing and works long hours to make ends meet.

This is where Alexandria meets people who, just like her, do not agree with American politics. They believe that both the Republicans and the Democrats are doing a tremendous disservice to the country. They decide they want to change that. In her native city of New York, Alexandria goes up against top Democrat Joe Crowley in the primary.

Nobody believes she has a chance, but Alexandria is unfazed. The months that follow are extremely hard work and riddled with challenges. Alexandria sees her waitressing experience as an advantage: 'If I was like a normal rational person, I would've dropped out of this race a long time ago. But my experience in hospitality has prepared me so well for this race. I'm used to being on my feet eighteen hours a day, I'm used to receiving a lot of heat. I'm used to people trying to make me feel bad. They call it 'working class' for a reason.'

In June 2018, something totally unexpected happens: Alexandria defeats her opponent. What a victory! Four months later she becomes the youngest woman ever to be elected to Congress. Alexandria is now a nationwide phenomenon. With her razor-sharp wit and intelligent clapbacks, she continues to fight for an inclusive country where everyone is treated equally and fairly, no matter where they come from.

Source: *Knock Down the House* (Netflix)

Alexandria Ocasio-Cortez is a go-getter. She doesn't give up when she is criticised or receives negative press. And she isn't afraid to call out critics. She has what is called 'grit'. Grit is a term that is used to describe courage or the will to get started. Grit is also about perseverance. To stick with it and to continue working hard even after experiencing failure. To pull yourself up by your bootstraps and start over. It's about resilience. Grit encompasses all these traits. Can grit be learned? Anything you can practise and get better at, even if it's only a little bit, can be defined as learnable. Including grit. So yes, grit is something you can develop.

There are always plenty of reasons to throw in the towel and raise the white flag of retreat. You're tired, it takes too much effort, there are more fun things to do, it's boring or you just don't feel like it.

There are also many good reasons not to want to make mistakes. People may think you're a loser. Or you're afraid to make mistakes because it makes you insecure or scared of what it will do to your reputation.

Whatever the reason, you should not give up but keep pushing. It will take you further.

16.1 What does research on perseverance tell us?

Research on grit shows that it helps to:
- Know that making mistakes does not mean that you are failing, but that you are learning.
- Know that taking your time does not mean that you are failing, but that you are learning.
- Accept that processing new information can be confusing and that's only natural.
- Accept that disappointment is a part of life.
- Accept boredom in your life every now and then.
- Know that short-term setbacks do not stand in the way of achieving your long-term goal.

Go-getters believe effort is the key to success and think of ways in which they can improve themselves. They are not concerned with what others think of them. Go-getters are motivated, whether the task is difficult or easy. They persevere, even when obstacles get in their way. They are inspired by other people's success. They have a clear idea of what their strengths are and what they need to work on.

You don't always need self-confidence to get things done. In fact, knowing that you're not the best can motivate you to try harder.

> **Go-getters know that mistakes don't define who you are**

Go-getters know that mistakes don't define who you are. Mistakes are an indication of where you are on the learning curve. Making mistakes is never fun, but it is not the end of the world. Mistakes show what skills or strategies you can improve by working on them and by learning from them.

16.2 Go-getters dare to make mistakes

I have failed my way to success.
– THOMAS EDISON

Allowing yourself to make mistakes is important. If you don't dare to make mistakes, you tend to avoid risks. This will limit your ability to learn. If you're not failing, you're not learning. Everyone makes mistakes. There is a Japanese proverb that says, 'Even monkeys fall from trees'.

This doesn't mean you should not feel disappointed or horrible when something goes wrong. There is, however, a difference between people who feel bad and wallow, and those who take action. Action instead of reaction. Do something instead of hiding. The story of Jim Marshall, a famous American football player who made a terrible mistake during an important match, is a prime example of this.

> **The wrong goal line**
>
> Jim Marshall scooped up the ball and ran with all his might in the opposite direction. Thinking that he had scored a touchdown for his team, he tossed the ball off the field in celebration. The crowd went wild. Unfortunately, they were cheering for his opponent. Marshall soon realised what he had done and felt so ashamed that he wanted the ground to open up and swallow him.
>
> Looking back on this moment he said, 'I realised I had a choice. I could wallow in my misery or I could do something about it. When you make a mistake, you have to put it right.' Marshall played an excellent second half and in this way contributed to his team's victory.
>
> But his story did not end there. He started giving lectures on this topic. And he has helped many people who were ashamed of their mistakes to overcome them and grow stronger.
>
> Source: Dweck, 2011, p. 33-34

16.3 Mistakes can lead to great discoveries

Very few inventions and discoveries were made entirely by chance on a lazy Sunday afternoon. If you read the biographies of great inventors, scientists and world travellers, you will see their path was full of difficulties and obstacles. They tried, made a lot of mistakes and started over. The mistakes did not prevent them from achieving their goals. On the contrary, they provided useful information. Many famous people have become the success story they are, not in spite of their mistakes but because of them.

A mistake does not constitute failure

Thomas Edison was one of the most productive inventors ever. He said, 'The path to my success is paved with failures'. The fact that he was almost entirely deaf from the age of 12 did not deter him. In fact, he used to claim that his deafness was an asset since it permitted him to concentrate on his work without being distracted. Edison ran a research laboratory, which eventually employed thousands of people at its peak. He patented 1,093 inventions, including the light bulb.

Some 70 years after the invention of electric light, Edison wanted to invent an affordable lamp that would last longer and be suitable for mass consumption. Actually, only one thing had to be discovered. The right thing to use for the filament, the material to convert electricity into light. That was all. The wire in the light bulb. Edison collected thousands of materials from all over the world, including all kinds of reeds and bamboo from the Amazon.

All these materials underwent the same treatment: they were charred, carefully placed in a vacuum glass and then

> assessed for their suitability to convert electricity into light. Often the material was of such poor quality that it fell apart even before the power was switched on.
>
> For years, Edison scoured the planet to find the perfect light bulb filament, a process which involved a large amount of donkey work. Until one day he achieved success with a charred cotton thread. The modern light bulb was born. Later Edison became famous for saying, 'I have not failed, not once. I have discovered 10,000 ways that don't work.'

Creative people tend to be more mistake-prone than others. This is because creative people try out different things before settling for something, and as a result, more things can go wrong. But unlike most of us, they value their mistakes as interesting. They learn from them. People can only develop through trial and error. This has nothing to do with being 'stupid' and everything to do with learning and growing.

16.4 Celebrate your mistakes

Many people are tired of a perfect 'Instagram-worthy' world. It is increasingly clear to us that we are fooling each other and ourselves. And that it's not the way to happiness or success.

The Museum of Failure does exactly the opposite. This travelling exhibition gets people to talk more openly about failure by putting failed corporate innovations on display: toothpaste brand Colgate's own brand of lasagne, the Betamax video

cassette recorder, Apple's first attempt at a tablet dubbed the Newton MessagePad, Heinz green or purple-coloured ketchup EZ Squirt, and Coca-Cola's Blak, a coffee-flavoured version of its signature product. Look up the museum on the web, it is a celebration of creative risk-taking.

Have you ever heard of Fuckup Nights? It all started in Mexico when a group of friends got drunk on mezcal and wondered why no one ever shares their failures. Since then, Fuckup Nights has grown into a global movement and event, where stories of failed businesses and projects are told, questioned and celebrated. It also has local chapters in the Netherlands.

There is also a moving development in medicine. More and more physicians, young and old alike, have the courage to be vulnerable and talk about their medical errors. Why? To learn from them. To help patients and their families come to terms with what has happened. And to help hospitals implement quality improvements so that similar errors can be prevented in the future.

> **Tips:**
> - Set challenging goals.
> - Dare to make mistakes.
> - When you make a mistake, consider what strategy or skill you could have used differently, and devise a plan based on this so that you can do things differently next time. Allow yourself to feel good when you accomplish what you've set out to do.
> - Be inspired by artists, top athletes, scientists, inventors, or people around you who have fallen flat on their faces but persevered and went on to achieve success.
> - Remember that it does not matter how deep you fall; what matters is how high you bounce back.

17 PRECONDITIONS

The final topic, preconditions, should be considered during every phase of the Circle of Learning Success. If you want to get even smarter, it is important to take care of yourself and your environment.

17.1 Your study environment

If your room, or whatever space you're using for studying, is neat and tidy you will be able to study faster and more effectively. An untidy room is distracting, in the same way that a room with lots of people is distracting. Clutter uses up capacity in the brain's working memory. A tidy room allows you to focus on the activity that truly matters, which is studying.

17.2 Take good care of your brain (and your body)

The brain is an integral part of the body, which is why it is important to take good care of it. Therefore, you should pay attention to the following points.

Fuel

Your brain consumes about 25% of all glucose in your body. Eating and drinking regularly will ensure your brain has enough fuel to keep it going. It's better not to snack on cookies, potato chips and energy drinks. When you consume quick-sugar foods, you will experience a brief sugar spike. But sugar spikes fade rapidly and are followed by a lull of low energy, the so-called 'glucose dip'. It is better to eat 'slow sugars' such as those found in fruit, vegetables and nuts. This will build up your energy without the infamous dip.

Take a break after you have eaten. To digest your food, all of your body's focus (i.e., blood) turns to the digestive organs.

This means that less energy is available to feed the brain. Once the digestive system is finished, oxygen and glucose can be transported to the brain again.

Oxygen

The brain's oxygen demands are enormous: it consumes approximately 20% of the oxygen we breathe. To ensure your brain gets sufficient oxygen to operate optimally, you can do the following:

- Open a window, stick out your head and take a couple of deep breaths.
- Go out for a short walk. Take a couple of deep breaths during your walk.
- Mind your breathing while you study. Breathe in through your nose, using your abdomen. Make sure your neck and shoulders are relaxed. When breathing in, you expand your abdomen slightly. It is very subtle, so don't overdo it. When breathing out, your abdomen becomes soft again and falls inwards.
- Stand up after every 20- to 45-minute block of studying. Stretch your body, and loosen your head, neck and shoulders. Take a few deep sighs. Jump up and down several times. This helps pump the oxygen through your body.

Regular relaxation

Give your brain regular breaks. Processing all the information that comes in takes time. Therefore, it is important to let it rest every now and then. How long it needs to rest depends on many things, such as the time of day, how long it has been since you ate, how bored you are or how difficult the study material is.

If you notice that you are no longer focussed, chances are your brain could do with a break. See for yourself how many minutes you need for your concentration to be back to normal. Then get back to work. If you can't get your concentration back, then you should stop for a bit longer.

17.3 The power of sleep

At night, the brain circuits you established or expanded during the day are further ingrained. Here are some things you can do to support this process:

- Avoid physical exercise at least one hour before bedtime.
- Switch off the TV, your computer and put away mobile devices at least one hour before going to bed.
- Avoid stress before going to sleep.
- Try not to eat, drink or smoke for two to three hours before going to bed.
- Do not use your bedroom, or in any case your bed, for studying, making phone calls or working on your laptop. And do not talk about problems in your bedroom or at bedtime.
- Make sure your bedroom is as dark, cool, well ventilated and quiet as possible.
- Once you are in bed, turn the alarm clock around so you can't see what time it is.
- Instead of counting sheep, imagine a relaxing scene, such as a soothing waterfall, and count drops of water. It's an effective aid to falling asleep.
- Try not to get anxious about not sleeping and just accept that at least you are resting your body.

Exercise – The worry list

If you don't make enough time during the day to brood calmly, you will take those worries to bed. This will affect the quality of your sleep, and you need a good night's sleep to be at your best. The networks that you established during the day are not only consolidated at night, you also process your emotions while you sleep.

If your mind is full of worries before you go to bed, it's no surprise you can't fall asleep. Here's a solution: create a worry list. In one column, write down all your problems. Then list possible solutions in a second column. Write down as many as you can think of. Take the time to imagine what the solutions would look like. Use as many of your senses as possible. What do you see, feel, hear, smell and experience when you think of this solution?

The funny thing with this exercise is that the solutions don't have to be brilliant. In fact, they can even be bad or absurd. No matter what, they will ensure that you fall asleep faster and sleep more soundly. Most likely, this is because you have got out of the 'worry mode'. The electrochemical activity in the brain circuits associated with the 'solutions mode' generate a different type of activity in your brain. This activity is beneficial for sleep.

18 A NEW ACTION PLAN

To conclude, let's go back to the beginning, to the Circle of Learning Success. We have discussed many things that can help you at various stages of studying. Now we are going to put all these pieces of the puzzle into the Circle, so that you can use them even more effectively.

Now that you have read everything, it's time to answer the following questions. What can you improve? And how? What do you do well and what could you do better?

Your personal top three

Look at the extended version of the Circle of Learning Success and name three things that you do well.

1. ....

2. ....

3. ....

THE CIRCLE OF LEARNING SUCCESS – THE EXTENDED VERSION

Work on:
- concentration difficulties
- problems with discipline
- motivation
- fear of failure
- procrastination

→ Attention

Optimise studying by:
- determining context
- investing in really understanding the material
- using certain study methods (e.g., mind mapping, alternating methods, mnemonics)

→ Establish new brain circuits

Take time to:
- revise
- practise
- explain out loud
- get a good night's sleep

→ Ingrain brain circuits

Make sure you:
- are in good shape
- have sufficient knowledge about the type of exam
- know what to do when you draw a blank
- are aware of the pitfalls of a resit

→ Exam or presentation

Be open to:
- finding out what you don't understand
- seeing your mistakes as opportunities for learning
- turning frustration into positive energy (mindset)
- asking for help

→ Evaluate results

Dare to:
- try a new method
- create a plan that works for you
- set priorities

→ Action plan

© Mirjam Pol

Make a mental note of these three things. Go back to them when you are studying. Think about how you can use them to your advantage. As you progress in your studies, you will learn new methods and tricks. Your toolkit will become fuller and fuller with new ways of thinking, feeling or doing. Or perhaps you will realise you need to stop doing something.

List three things you could do better (or even better):

1. ....

2. ....

3. ....

There is a difference between thinking of something you would like to improve or change, and actually doing it. To get things done you need to take action. But taking action can be difficult. If you would like to be more action oriented, it helps to be as specific as possible.
- How many times a week will you work on it?
- When exactly?
- How much time a day or week will you dedicate to it?
- What exactly will you be doing?
- When are you going to start?
- How will you know you are on the right track?
- How will you track your progress?
- How often will you track your progress?
- How do you plan to deal with setbacks?

Make a list of activities you will do, when you will do them, and how long they will last.

This is the last chapter. You have learned so much! For instance, to look at learning as a process of organising and re-organising networks in your brain. And that learning is a logical, step-by-step process. You have also learned that you can guide this process through practice, motivation, enjoyment, reviewing and perseverance. You have been given a range of study techniques and methods that you can experiment with. You know how to make a study plan to manage your time effectively. You can track your progress and adjust your plan if you need to. And you can do so again and again. This way, you will continue to learn, grow and develop throughout your life. And get smarter every day!

TIPS FOR BOOKS AND VIDEOS

Books
David Allen, *Getting things done – The Art of Stress-free Productivity*.
Tony Buzan, *Mind Map Mastery*.
Carol Dweck, *Mindset – How we can learn to fulfil our potential*.
Joshua Foer, *Moonwalking with Einstein – The Art and Science of Remembering Everything*.
Malcolm Gladwell, *Outliers – The Story of Success*.
Paul Loomans, *Time Surfing*.
John Medina, *Brain Rules*.
Mirjam Pol, *From Stress to Success*.

YouTube
Brain Power: From Neurons to Networks.
TEDx Max Cynader: Enhancing the Plasticity of the Brain.
TEDx Joshua Foer: Feats of Memory Anyone Can Do.
TEDx Adam Gazzaley: Brain: Memory and Multitasking.

Netflix:
Knock Down the House (documentary), directed by Rachel Lears.

This book has helped you lay the foundation for successful learning. If you would like to learn more about dealing with study stress (brooding, fear of failure, perfectionism, writer's block, public speaking anxiety), you may find *From Stress to Success. A Practical Guide for Students* useful.

Books by Mirjam Pol available from VU University Press:

Nog slimmer! Succesvol studeren aan de universiteit
Nog slimmer! Succesvol studeren aan de hogeschool
Get Smarter! Set Yourself Up for Study Success
Van stress naar succes. Praktische wegwijzer voor studenten
From Stress to Success. A Practical Guide for Students

For questions or comments, please contact us via
info@vuuniversitypress.nl